An Account of the Genea-
logy of the Family
of Loraine.

REPRINTED BY M. A. RICHARDSON,
IN GREY STREET, NEWCASTLE.
MDCCCXLVIII.

ONLY 100 COPIES PRINTED.

The Contents of this Book.

The wayfarings of Ralph Thoresby in the North of England: being such portions of the Diary and Correspondence of the Historian of Leeds, as relate to the North of England, with copious local annotation.

The humble Petition and Appeal of Thomas Cliffe, a poor Shipwright, inhabiting at North Shields, to the supream authority of the Nation, the Commons assembled in Parliament.

An Answer to the Proclamation of the Rebels of the North, mdlxix. From a black-letter copy in the public library of the University at Cambridge.

Such account of the ancient and honourable family of Loraine of Kirkharle as Collins gave, was printed, with some alterations, in four pages folio, with this title: "A short account of the genealogy and other memoirs concerning the family of Loraine, sometimes antiently written Lorein, of Kirkharle-tower, in the county of Northumberland, anno Domini, m.d.ccxij:" which account was reprinted in the same size, and again in mdccxl in twenty pages octavo. It is from this latter edition, now grown very scarce, that we have made our present reprint, as it presents a highly curious narrative pedigree of the race, seemingly derived from an inspection of the family muniments, and that probably, by a lawyer whose name, however, we have been unable to discover.

The copy whence our reprint is derived was kindly placed in our hands by Thomas Burnet, esq., but an erasure had been made at the termination of the paragraph relating to the election of Sir William Loraine, as representative in Parliament for the county of Northumberland in mdcc (see p. xviij, line x). Since printing off our copy, thus imperfect, we have fallen in with another copy of the tract, and are now enabled to give the paragraph entire thus: "He was chosen a member of the House of Commons for the said county, in the reign of King William, purely by the Love of his Country, and the favour of the Duke of Somerset."

The Journals of the House of Commons inform us that Bertram Stote, esq. who was a third candidate at that election, complaining, by a petition to the House, bij January, mdccij, that many unqualified persons were permitted to poll against him, and that Mr. Loraine, by illegal practices of himself and agents, and also of the high-sheriff, was unduly returned; the petition was referred to the committee of privilege and elections, and Mr. Loraine declared unduly elected.

Ay. A. R. at Newcastle, this Julye,
mdccexlviij.

An Account of the

GENEALOGY,

AND OTHER

·MEMOIRS

Concerning the FAMILY of

L O R A I N E,

OF

KIRKHARLE-TOWER IN THE *County of*
NORTHUMBERLAND;

WITH

REMARKS upon some others,
(obiter) Anno Dom. 1738.

NEWCASTLE:
Printed by J O H N W H I T E.

MDCCXL.

AN

ACCOUNT

OF THE

Genealogy, *and other* Memoirs,

CONCERNING

The Family of *LORAINE,* of *Kirkharle-Tower,* in the County of *Northumberland ;* with Remarks upon some others, *(obiter) Anno Dom.* 1738.

Robert, the first of this Family in *Eng-land,* came an Officer in the Army of *William* the Conquerer, who, for his Service in that Expedition, and after in the sixth Year of the Reign of his Son *William* II. against *Malcolm* King of *Scots,* (a valiant Prince) whom the *English* Rebels in the North join'd in his Excurtion into *Northumberland,* whereby many Estates in that County and *Durham* were forfeited to the Crown, was rewarded with several Hides of Land in *Ufferton, East, Middle* and *West Harrington;* with free Fishings in *Aqua de Were,* to him and his Heirs for ever, to be holden in Knights Service :

Where he settled himself and Family, and whose Descendants intermarried with some of the ancient and chief Families of the Gentry in that County.

He was (as well as a Soldier) a considerable Scholar for that age; as recorded in *Baker's Chronicle,* amongst the Men of Note in that Reign, for epitomizing the Chronicle of *Marianus Scotus.*

He lived in the said County of *Durham* till the Reign of Henry V. about which Time there was one *William del-Strother,* presum'd of the Natives and ancient Inhabitants of the County of *Northumberland,* who was a Man of great Power and Possessions, and had his chief Seat and Mansion-house at *Kirkharle-Tower* in the said County, distant fourteen miles from *Newcastle-upon-Tyne;* situate upon the Bank, and over-looking a spacious Lake ; surrounded with Timber and Under-wood; interspersed with Apertures, Lawns and Savanas ; cloathed with the finest Herbage :

Which *William Del-Strother* died without Issue-male, leaving only three Daughters, *viz. Johanna,*

Alicia, and *Maria*, to whom all his Estate descended; who, out of their Piety and Devotion, at their joint Expence, repair'd the Church of *Kirkharle*, then under a Decay; standing from their Father's House about a Furlong:

Which *Johanna*, eldest Daughetr and Co-heir of the said *Strother*, *William Loraine*, Heir of this Family, married, having then a considerable Estate in the County of *Durham*: By whom he had Issue Sons and Daughters.

Alicia, the second Daughter and Co-heir, married one *John Nicholson* in the County of *Northumberland*.

John Fenwick, of *Fenwick-Tower* in *Northumberland*, married *Maria*, the third Daughter and Co-heir of the said *Strother;* who with their three Wives, enjoy'd all the said Estate, in common and undivided, till the said *Nicholson*, with his wife and Son, released all their Right and Title to the Father's Estate to *Loraine* and *Fenwick;* in consideration of having for their Share thereof the Manor of *Babington*, alias *Bavington, cum membris;* whereof *Thockrington* is specially nam'd.

Note, *It is presum'd, the* Shaftoes *got the said Manor of* Babington *by a Match with the Heiress of the* Nicholsons; *because no mention is made of that Family after.*

Whereupon *Loraine* and *Fenwick* made a Partition

of the rest of the Estate betwixt them, whereby the *Tower* (being the chief Seat of the said *Strother*) the Manor, and Lordship of *Kirkharle*, with the Advowson of the Church, was allotted to *Johanna* (in Preference to the eldest Co-heir) with about nineteen Hundred Acres of arable Land (except about two Hundred thereof rocky, moorish, or marshy) with the Members thereof, *viz*. the said Tower, Township and Village of *Kirkharle*, *Great-law*, &c. all situate on the South-side of the River *Wansbeck*.

And *John Fenwick* had the other half of the Estate for his Part, *cum membris*, *viz*, the Tower, Manor and Lordship of *Wallington*, *Sweethop*, *Hawick*, *Crookden*, &c. lying mostly on the North-side of the said River.

Note, The Ancestors of the Strothers *got the Estate of* Wallington *with* Johanna *the sole Heir, and Daughter of* Robert de Wallington East, *and* Wallington West; *(as express'd in the ancient Deeds).*

After which Marriage, the said *William Loraine* removed out of the County of *Durham*, with his Family, to his Wife's Estate at *Kirkharle* aforesaid; whose Posterity intermarried with several of the reputable and ancient Families of both the said Counties, who, by the prudent Management of their Affairs, acquired other Estates there; some of Lands of Inheritance, Coal-mines; others consisting of Chattels, Ecclesiastical Leases, &c. Being in their respective Generations generally Men of Learning, Virtue and Sobriety.

EDWARD succeeded, who married *Elizabeth*, the Daughter of *John Harding* of *Hallinside* in the County of *Durham*, Esq ; By whom he had several Children, and died the End of the Reign of *Richard* III.

ROBERT came in by Descent, and was so zealous a Prosecutor of Robbers, Thieves, and Moss-troopers, (called the *Border-service*) that he kept a certain Number of Horses and Arms always ready, suitable to his Estate: As others of the chiefest Families in the Neighbourhood did; as *Fenwick* of *Wallington*, *Swinburne* of *Capheaton*, *Middleton* of *Belsay*, *Shaftoe* of *Babington*, &c. to pursue the same, upon all Occasions of theirs and the *Scots* Excursions and Depredations into *Northumberland*.

For which Service to his Country, they conceived such a Malice to him, that a Party of them lay in Ambush, between his House and the Church (where he frequently resorted for his private Devotions) and in his Return home, suddenly surprised and dragg'd him into an adjacent Close, where they barbarously murdered him.

In memory whereof, his Successor set up a great Stone in the Place, which the present Gentleman finding defac'd, and broken down, erected a new one in its Place, engraven with the same Account.

This unfortunate Gentleman about the fourteenth of *Henry* VIII. married *Margaret* Daughter of *Robert Bowes* of the Bishoprick of *Durham*, Esq; and had Issue Sons and Daughters.

WILIAM succeeded, and married *Agnes*, a Daughter of Sir *William Waters* of the County of *York*, Knight; who became a Widow, and married *John Lisle* of *Acton* in *Northumberland*, Esq; By which *Agnes*, the said *William* had Issue one Son and two Daugters, *Thomas, Ursilla* and *Dorothy;* which *Dorthy* married *Thomas Ogle* of *Kirkley* in *Northumberland*, Esq;.

THOMAS came in by Descent, and married *Thomasin*, eldest Daughter of *Thomas Walter* of *Whitwell* in the County of *Durham*, Gentleman; and died the fifteenth of *Jacobi Regis*, leaving two Sons, *Thomas* and *William*, Infants: Whose Widow married *John Hylton* in the County of *Durham*, Esq;.

THOMAS succeeded, and married *Elizabeth*, Widow and Relict of *Thomas Bewick* of *Close-house* in *Northumberland*, Esq; By whom he had Issue only one Son, called *Thomas*.

The said *Thomas* the Father, out of his Piety, finding the slated Roof of the Quire of *Kirkharle* Church fallen into Decay, took it down, and timber'd it a-new with *Irish* Oak, and cover'd it with Lead; all at his own charge: And some Time after prevail'd with the Parishoners to take down the slated Roof of the Church, and timber'd it with Oak, and cover'd the same with Lead also.

He was likewise so great a Lover of Learning (though then the sole male Heir of his Family) that he continued with that learned Gentleman, Mr. *Mede* of *Christs-College*, *Cambridge*, in Pursuit thereof, that he was reputed as great a Proficient in the *Latin*, *Greek* and *Hebrew* Tongues, as any Layman in that University.

He was so loyal and serviceable to the King (as his Ancestors had been) that a Party of *Oliver's* Soldiers burnt a small Seat-house of his, and seven or eight more belonging to it, to the Ground in *Ufferton* aforesaid.

His great Learning and Endowments brought him into so great an Esteem and Familiarity with *Cozens*, then Bishop of *Durham*, that he stood God-father to his said Son *Thomas*, to whom he gave a handsome Present of a Silver Censer upon that Occasion.

He was a proper Person, and of a comely Aspect; a virtuous, sober, honest Man. He lived and died of a Fever in *Newcastle upon Tyne*, in the thirty fifth Year of his Age, to the great Grief and Loss of his Family and Relations, and Regret of his Acquaintance, and was interred in the South Isle of St. *Nicolas's* Church, next the *Maddison's* Monument, under a large Marble Stone, with a Brass Plate, and his Character engraven upon it (which being torn up and stol'n) the present Gentleman put a new one upon it, engraven with the same Character.

His Wife died some Years after, and was buried next to him in the same Place (who being the last surviving Person of the *Maddison's* Family) the Right of the said Monument and Burying-place devolved upon the *Loraine's* Family.

THOMAS his Son succeeded, who married *Grace,* (a comely, prudent and careful Woman) the eldest Daughter of Sir *William Fenwick* of *Walmington* in the County of *Northumberland,* Baronet, who was the eldest Son of *Grace Loraine* of this Family (reputed a Beauty) second Wife of Sir *John* his Father, [for this *vide* the *Fenwick's Pedigree.*] who brought him Issue fourteen Sons and five Daughters.

He was created Baronet the twenty-sixth Year of King *Charles* II. and died *January* 1717, aged near Eighty, and was interr'd in the Chancel of *Kirkharle* Church.

WILLIAM his first born Son, the present Gentleman, succeeded, and was educated to the Law at *Lincoln's-Inn,* where he took his Degree of Barrister, and practised the same for several Years, till the

Affairs of his Family required his Presence at home to attend the same.

He married two Wives; the first *Elizabeth*, one of the Daughters of Sir *John Lawrence*, Knight and Alderman of the City of *London*, (Lord Mayor in the *Sickness Year* call'd) who died in three Years, leaving him no Issue.

His second Wife was *Anne*, only Daughter of *Richard Smith* of *Preston* in the County of *Bucks*, Esq; and Sister to *Richard Smith* of *Enderby* in the County of *Leicester*, Esq; who followed King *Charles* II. Beyond Sea all the Time of his Misfortunes and Exile; and returned with him at his Restoration, was made Clerk of the Cheque: In which Place he behaved himself so well, that he was continued therein till his Death.

By whose Daughter, now living, he had Issue five Sons and four Daughters; whereof there are now living two Sons and two Daughters.

His Daughter *Grace* was married to *Forster Charleton* of *Lee-hall* in the County of *Northumberland*, Gentleman; who died leaving him Issue three Sons and one Daughter.

He married *Charles* his younger Son to Miss *Margaret Lambton*, sister to *Henry Lambton* in the County of *Durham*, Esq;.

He was made Justice of Peace for *Northumberland*

in the Reign of *William* and *Mary*, and hath been continued so, through all the Reigns since, to the present.

He was made a Deputy-Lieutenant there, by *Richard* Earl of *Scarborough*, in the eighth Year of King *William* III. which was renewed by the same Earl the first of Queen *Anne*.

He was chosen a Member of the House of Commons for the said County in the Reign of King *William*, purely by the Love of his Country.

He is competent in Judgment, of Architecture and Physick, exemplary in Planting and Inclosure; having from the Year 1694 to 1738 *inclusive*, planted of Forest-Trees Twenty four thousand, and of Quick-Sets above Four hundred and eighty eight thousand; and being skilful in the Fruit-Garden, planted of Fruit-Trees Five hundred and eighty.

Who by his various Industry besides; as dividing the Grounds, building new Farms upon them, draining Morasses, clearing the Lands of ponderous, massy and hard Stones, to prepare them for Tillage; By which Means (with the Assistance of his Wives Portions) he hath redeemed a good Part of his Estate, adding some others to it of his own Purchase. By struggling with, and the assiduous Application of above fifty Years, he hath reduced his Family to pretty easy Circumstances, from difficult and numerous Troubles and Incumbrances.

He pav'd with Free-Stone all the Quire of *Kirk-harle* Church, (before an Earthen Floor) arch'd the East Window, coop'd and repair'd the Roof, Pillars and Walls thereof; made an Altar-Rail, built a new Pulpit, set upon a hewn Pillar of Stone, a Desk, four new Pews, for himself and Family, and two in the Church: And by his good Example and Persuasion, prevail'd with the Parishoners to pave the Church with Free-stone also, and make decent Pews throughout the same.

He likewise built the West Gable, Porch, and Bell-Cope, (all ruinous) at his own Charge.

He also built a new Mansion-house (of his own Plan and Contrivance) with all the Offices, Out-Houses, Gardens, Fountains, Fish-Ponds, &c, (the first regular ones ever were in that Country) belonging to them.

The Heirs of the Family having the Misfortune, during those dreadful and pernicious Times of Court of Wards and Liveries, of falling three Times successively into Wardship, *viz*, *William* in the Twenty sixth of Queen *Elizabeth*, at eighteen Years old; *Robert* in the Thirty fifth of the said Queen, at two Years old and eight months; *Thomas* in the Reign of King *James*, at two Years old, were defrauded by covetous and perfidious Guardians, and others, from time to time, of several considerable Members of their Estates, in both the said Counties.

And particularly the present Gentleman's Predecessor, by his imprudent Credulity, was circumvented and defrauded of one, to the Amount of the best Part of Twenty thousand Pounds; by a certain Gentleman (whose honourable and laudable Character (ιιΡαινία) was *Double tongued Jemmy*, in an ancient and worthy Corporation in the North, which he lived near, where *William Rufus* finished a Castle (pardon the *Ænigma*). And this he practised under the greatest Confidence, Trust, and seeming Friendship imaginable, and the Relation of an Uncle.

Note, Naboth's *Vine-yard ; the Estate lying near his own House.*

The truth is, he was a Man of good Parts, which he studiously employ'd to accomplish his worldly Interest, *quoquomodó* an Allegator of Mens Estates, as experienced by those who had the Misfortune to deal with him *de terris & tenementis.*

The Author of this Collection, upon Perusal of many ancient Deeds in the Possesion of the Family, finds it Owners of Estates and Effects, now, and in former Generations, *viz.* in the county of *Durham,* their original Estates in *England;* as *Ufferton, South-Field, East, Middle* and *West Harrington,* with free Fishings in *Aqua de Were, Wode-Hall,* Lands and Houses in *Chester le Street, Whitwell, Pancher, Byer moor* and *Collery,* and another at *Ryton.*

And within the Verge and Boundery of *Northumberland*, Lands and Houses in *Cramlington*, *Slate-Houses*, *Chapington*, *Hunt-Law*, a third part of *Frewick*, *Low-Hall*, with the half of the Village of *Great-Bavington*, and the Lands and Tenements thereunto belonging; The said Manor and Lordship of *Kirkharle* with all the Lands and Tenements thereunto belonging (which is holden of the Crown, as a Member of the Barony of *Bolbeck*, by a Yearly Rent of four Shillings and eight Pence) and the Rectory of *Kirkharle* Church, with the perpetual Advowson thereof (which is also holden of the Crown in free Socage of the Manor of *East-Greenwich*, *per* annual Rent of three Pounds three Shillings and four Pence.

Which, by reason, of the many Alienations, Frauds, Lapse of Time for the Recovery of them, Loss of Evidences in the Times of the national Troubles and Disturbances, with some bad Conduct in the last Generation, several considerable Branches of the Estate were lopp'd off, to the great Diminution of the Funds and Effects of the Family.

There have been two considerable military Men of the Family buried in the Chancel of the said Church, which appears by two long Stones lying there ; one engraven, with a large long Sword on the Sinister, and a Staff, and plain Escutcheon fix'd to it, in the Middle ; and on the other, a Staff, with a large long

Sword also, on the Sinister, engraven, with handsome Flourishes on the Top of each Staff: Which Dr. *Hunter, Herald at Arms,* supposes to have been Knights-Templars of *the Order of St. John of Jerusalem.* Given under his Hand.

I have subjoin'd the Coat of Arms of the Family, with the Crest and Motto blazon'd ; by which it appears to have been obtained by some Action in the Field of Battle, for which there is the Authority of Tradition in the Family, and what is implied in the Crest and Motto themselves.

*IT beareth Quarterly Sable, and Argent, a Plain Cross
Counterquarter'd on the Field, borne up by a Laurel-
tree Coop'd; Two Branches sprouting out proper, and
fix'd to the Lower thereof, with a Belt Gules, Edg'd
and Buckl'd, Or.*

Letters of William Scott father of lords Stowell and Eldon. 1745-48.

IMPRINTED BY M. A. RICHARDSON,
IN GREY STREET, NEWCASTLE.
MDCCCXLVIII.

ONLY 100 COPIES PRINTED.

TO

WILLIAM JOHN FORSTER, ESQUIRE,

A DESCENDANT OF HIM

WHO IS HEREIN CHIEFLY COMMEMORATED,

THE FOLLOWING EXTRACTS

FROM HIS MERCANTILE CORRESPONDENCE

ARE DEDICATED BY THE EDITOR.

lthough the letters here given hardly extend over four years, and are chiefly confined to the business transactions of the writer, there is yet sufficient highly to interest us, seeing that he was the father of two of the most accomplished lawyers who ever graced the judicial bench. We do not find it necessary, therefore, to urge any apology for the publication of these letters, though we hope to have at least, not lessened their value and interest, by our illustrative notes and extracts from cotemporaneous letter-writers. The volume whence we have obtained our copy is in the MS. library of John Bell, esq. of Gateshead, to whom we are indebted for its use.

M. A. R. at Newcastle, this August, mdccclviij.

reat and manifold are the difficulties which beset the inquirer after the history of names possessing community of origin: were the name of Scott among the favoured number whose uniqueness of rise, singularity of construction, rarity, locality, restriction of range, or any other attaching peculiarity calculated to render the tracing of descents and connections a matter of comparative ease, it would indeed impart to us high gratification, insomuch as it would afford an opportunity rightly to deduce the descent of a race of men whose posterity have ennobled their line, and conferred no little honour on the town wherein they first drew breath and received the good seeds of their intellectual culture. With the name of Scott, however, we are sorely beset: search as

we will, and accumulate as many piles of extracts
from this, that, or the other musty deposit, as we
may, we cannot find anything satisfactorily to prove
connection ; paucity of material might readily be
supposed to *impede* it, but here their very number
defies it, for the number of families bearing the name
is incalculable. Equally difficult therefore, is it, to
determine at what period to commence, at which to
take up, or where to branch out. Equally uncer-
tain too, is the very origin of the name : an
extensive clan in the south of Scotland is called
Scot because of their being Scotch, in contradistinction to the *English* borderers whom they immediately adjoin ;—these, however, even in early
times, had assumed the appelative as a transmissible
and family name ; but further south, another source
for the name early got rise—should an adventurous
Caledonian by any chance or good luck manage to
ensconce himself on the south side of the Tweed (and
in these days it was no easy feat to effect) no matter
what name he bore in his fatherland, he is called by
his adopted brethren " the Scot," or as it frequently
occurs " le Scot." An instance of this class is to be
found in the knightly family of Calverley als Scot,
which also exhibits the manner in which a new name
was assumed, though it shows the difficulty of getting rid of the former appelative, which in this family
wavered for a great length of time, in the contest be-

tween the national and the territorial cognomen. This was Alphonso, the son of Gospatric, first mesne lord of Calverley and Pudsey in the county of York; whose younger daughter, Laderina, married one John, who from his country was named Scoticus or Scot, (he coming out of Scotland with Maude, the empress, as steward of her household) ; and his descendants, though really *de Calverley* did not drop the *alias* until about the reign of Henry the Seventh.[a] The acute schoolman Duns Scotus too, received his name from Englishmen, in respect of his northern origin, (for we may not any longer contend for his Northumbrian *birth*, if we may for his education) and we feel justified in attributing a like origin to Sirs Peter and Nicholas Scot, the first who held the office of mayor in Newcastle-upon-Tyne. Thus we might adduce instance upon instance, but they work little or nothing for our present purpose—they will not supply us with any assistance towards the finding of a likely ancestor for *our* race of Scotts, so we must resort to presumptive evidence for argument.

[a] Even so late as 1406, (one whom we believe to have been) the then representative of the family of de Calverley, made his will in the name of "Johannes Scot, miles," and it is singular to observe how unsettled family names remained up to a much later period. The issue of Philip Thirlwall, migrating to the lakes to the west of the antient castle and domain of his forefathers, founded a new family under the name of Philip*son*, from whom descend the present family of Ralph Park Philipson, esq., and his late brother Nicholas John Philipson, a zealous heraldic antiquary, both of Newcastle-upon-Tyne.

We find a family of this name which seems to have resided chiefly in Sandgate, and to have affected a river-side and colliery employment at least from the days of Charles the First; and reasoning from the facts, that this particular family does not appear to occur at all in the reign of Elizabeth, and the name of Scott by whomsoever borne, at that period, but seldom, it is far from improbable that the race in question were of the Lowland family of the name, and of the vast number of Scottish adventurers who came in with James the Sixth of Scotland, when about to become the First of the name in England.

Affecting a river-side employment, therefore, appears readily to suggest a river-side residence, and as the family to which we allude were not free of the town, and possibly not on the very best of terms with the inhabitants within the walls, they in all probability at their first coming, adopted as a place of residence, the eastern suburbs of the town without the Sand-gate, which has ever since been the resort of strangers and unfree: Sandgate, however, to this day, bears traces of a race of occupants much superior to the present. There are many of the houses of the Carolan or Oliverian period quite equal in build and aspect to any within the town of a like date, and it is evident that there have resided in Sandgate, men of the best worldly position.

There was living, probably in this place, in 1662, one John Scott who "fitted" the coles of Miles Man, hostman, whom we apprehend to have been the father of William Scott, the keel-owner, who was certainly the parent of William Scott the Host-man, and subject of our tract.

William Scott,[b] described as the son of " William Scott of Sandgate in the county of Northumberland, yeoman," was apprenticed for seven years to Thomas Brummell, junior, hostman, on 1 Sep. 1716 ;[c] but on

[b] We are inclined to think that William, the hostman, had an elder brother, as a "James son of William Scott of Newcastle, yeoman," was apprenticed to Francis Collinson, hostman, on 7 Feb. 1704, for the space of seven years ; but on 13 May, 1713, the fraternity ordered him to be crossed out of the books and to be debarred freedom, he having absented his master's service, and not duly serving him when with him. What became of this James, we have not yet seen.—*Hostmen's books.*)

[c] Thomas Brumell was the son of Thomas Brumell of Braithwaite, co. Cumberland, yeoman, apprenticed to sir William Blackett II., hostman, on 14 Oct. 1684, and admitted to freedom ou 23 Aug. 1700. Brumell appears to have held a high place in the esteem of his master, and to have acted as the steward or manager of the affairs of his son and successor in the baronetcy, sir William III ; in which also, Thomas Brumell, junior, appears to have shared, and probably acted in the capacity of secretary to sir William while attending his parliamentary duties in London. In 1733, the elder Brummell gave bond to the Cordwainers in forty pounds, to pay twenty shillings a day for every day, he, his daughter, or servants should expose to sale or sell any sort of women's and children's shoes or slippers within Newcastle or its liberties, or otherwise exercise the art of a cordwainer, except in the sale of clogs !" We trust that our hostman did not dabble in shoe leather in his own person ; Brumell however, must now have been getting old, and it is probable his income was sought to be eked out by the exertions of his wife and daughter—though, as we may observe, the cordwainers soon set their faces against it.

4 Jan. 1718, was set over, on his petition, to Joseph Colpitts.*d* He was admitted to the freedom of this fraternity on 7 Sep. 1724, when he gave the usual, but optional dole of five shillings to the poor.*e*

Dr. Surtees, in alluding to the degree of *yeoman* by which, in the deed of his son's apprenticeship,

---

d Of the family of Colpitts of Newcastle, we may remark that Roger Colpitts of Longnewton, co. Dur. gentleman, who probably died between 1 Nov. 1692 and 1 Ap. 1702, was its progenitor.

His son Lyonell, (apprenticed to Joseph Atkinson, hostman, 1 Nov. 1692, admitted to the freedom of that fraternity 9 Feb. 1699, and died just previous to 15 June, 1716), was, by Alice his wife, (buried 10 March, 1729-30) the father of

George Colpitts, who was sheriff in 1743-4, and the latter part of 1781-2. He was admitted to the hostmen by patrimony, 2 July, 1742, died 30 Oct. 1795, and was buried in the chancel of Long Benton, where there is a slab to his memory. He bought Killingworth Hall of John Williams (son of John Williams the glass-owner, who built it) and made large additions thereto, as did Joseph Reay, (son of alderman Henry Reay,) who married his niece. In 1763, he gave a chalice to the church of Long Benton. He was admitted to the honorary freedom of the House Carpenters in his second shrievalty, on 5 Sep. 1782. He voted for Ridley and Delaval in 1780, at which time he is described as residing in Newcastle.

Joseph Colpitts (brother of Lyonell, and a younger son of Roger) was apprenticed to John Swaddell, hostman, on 1 Ap. 1702, admitted to the freedom of the fraternity, 12 Aug. 1709: he died 27 May, 1729, aged 41 years, and was buried in the north aisle of the old church of All Saints, two days after,—" opus manserit et mercedem accipiet." He married at S. Nicholas, on 20 Feb. 1717, Elizabeth, widow of . . . . Shepherd. We believe that another of George Colpitts' nieces married Admiral Roddam.—*(Hostmens' and Ho. Carp's. books,—Regs. All Saints and S. Nich.—Hornby MS.—Spearman MS. —Brand.—Besly Des. Not.—Poll Books, &c.)*

e His companions in apprenticeship were John, son of William Ladler of Swalwell, co. Dur. yeoman, apprenticed to George Smales, 2 Dec. 1716, but 20 May, 1717, set over by consent to Joseph Colpitts, and admitted free 4 Jan. 1724;—Robert, son of George Noble of Whitby, master and mariner, apprenticed to Joseph Colpitts, 11 Oct. 1721;—James, son of John Walker, at the time of apprentice-

the father is called, excellently defines it, " a style not necessarily signifying the cultivator of his own farm, as we commonly understand it; [but] there is no doubt simply meaning a householder, of too poor estate to allow of his designation either as a gentleman or merchant, yet raised above the ranks of servile drudgery. It was applied alike to the reduced cadets of gentle blood, and to the aspiring scions of the successful labourer. The history of the family of Scott," he proceeds " well exemplifies the quaint definition which the venerable Fuller has given of the class comprised under this term—' the good yeoman is a gentleman in ore, whom the next age may see refined ; and is the wax capable of a gentle impression when the Prince shall stamp it.' "*ʃ*

Lord Eldon himself said before the Pitt Club, in opposing the Reform bill as agitated in 1831, " The aristocracy once destroyed, the best supporters of the lower classes would be swept away. In using the term lower classes he meant nothing offensive. How could he do so ? He himself had been one of the

ship described as late of Wylam, co. Northd. gentleman, deceased, apprenticed to George Headlam on 14 Dec. 1722, but on the same day set over to Joseph Colpitts,—and, Robert, son of William Hudspeth of Corbridge, co. Northd. gentleman, apprenticed to William Emmerson, 2 Jan. 1722, but set over to Joseph Colpitts.

ʃ Sketch of the Lives of Stowell and Eldon, by W. E. Surtees, D.C.L., page 3.

lower classes. He gloried in the fact, and it was noble and delightful to know that the humblest in the realm might, by a life of industry, propriety, and good moral and religious conduct, rise to eminence. All could not become eminent in public life,—that was impossible; but every man might arrive at honour, independence, and competence.*"

Our hostman had his due share of the duties of the fraternity, and appears to have fulfilled them in every particular: On 4 Jan. 1725, he was first elected one of the seizors of unfreemens' coals,—an unpleasant office to which young brethren were usually appointed previous to their holding any other of higher character. This post he held for three consecutive years. On 4 Dec. 1734, he was appointed one of the committee for considering the expediency of abolishing the qualification of absolute ownership of coal on the part of those free of the company, as indispensable to the taking of apprentices. It appears probable that their deliberations were unfavourable to any alteration in the existing order, as it was never formally repealed.* We cannot however, from this circumstance, imply that Scott was the owner of a colliery either in one shape or another, neither does he mention any such property in his will. It is probable however that laxity

*Twiss, iij. 127.   *Hostmen's books.

of rule shortly crept in, as Scott occurs taking apprentices from the year 1740.[i] On 4 Jan. 1739, he was appointed one of the auditors of the company's accounts, an office which he held *in perpetuum*, till his last election 4 Jan. 1768, having for the terminal three years of officership been the senior of the three annually elected.

" The family of Scott," remarks Dr. Surtees, " may be considered as owing their rise from a humble condition more to the patronage of the great Durham house of Bowes of Gibside than to any other source, always excepting the blessing of Providence upon their own honourable industry."[j] This remark we have found to be in direct accordance with many portions of the correspondence we print, as also with the following passage in a letter from George Bowes himself,[k] who, writing from Gibside, 15 March,

---

[i] William Scott's apprentices were Philip Dunn, 2 Jan. 1740, and Creighton Dawson apprenticed on 1 Feb. 1755. This latter youth, however, on or about January, 1755, deserted his master's service, and on 13 Oct. 1757, Scott came to the court then sitting, and desired that his apprentice might be crossed out of the book of inrollment.—(*Hostmen's books.*)

[j] Surtees' Sketch, 45.

[k] George Bowes of Gibside, esq. He was apprenticed for seven years on 14 Dec. 1731 to Anthony Tullie, hostman, when his father, sir William Bowes, of Streatlam Castle, knight, is described as then deceased. On 29 Nov. in the ensuing year, he was by consent of the company, set over to Henry Atkinson, in consequence of Tullie's death. Bowes does not appear to have himself assumed the freedom, but employed Scott and others to " fit" his coals, at the same

1723-4 to Mr. Gibson, apparently acting in London as his agent there, says, "I hope I have so settled all my coal affairs in y⁰ countrey, that my commodity will both come clean and round to the market, and do not doubt your diligence in giving them their deserved character. I have made great alterations amongst my fitters, and believe very much to my advantage and to their satisfaction. I may safely say that I have *the best and honestest fitters in Newcastle,* *viz:* *Mr. Scott,* (who is to be only servant under Alderman Fenwick and partners,) Mr. Simpson, Mr. Henry Atkinson, and Selby, the latter being upon his good behaviour."[1]

Scott, at this time, however, was not free of his company, and the only way we can reconcile the state-

time keeping up a friendly intercourse with the rest of the fraternity, as exemplified in the following extract, "paid Mr. Bowes' servant when he brought venison 10s." During the repair and alteration of Gibside, Bowes rented Ledston, near Wakefield, at 104*l.* per annum. The lease dated from 17 Oct. 1741.

Bowes' apprenticeship to Tullie, we apprehend, was not a mere matter of chance, but resulted from an amount of relationship which subsisted between them—kinsmen they were, though we have not our pedigrees by us at this moment to show to what extent they were so. Thomas Tullie, rector of Middleton in Teesdale and of Romald Kirk, became the second husband of Elizabeth, daur. of Thomas Bowes, sister to Sir Talbot Bowes; her first spouse having been *Timothy* Hutton of Marske, co. Ebor., from which second marriage came, among others, *Timothy* Tullie, a Newcastle merchant. They were of the same stock as the Tullies of Carlisle, and of S. Nicholas, Newcastle, so notable in the church history of the time of James II.—*Hostmen's books, Sharp MSS., &c.*

[1] Sharp MSS.

ment of the letter is to suppose that the appointment was prospective, and made in the expectation of his taking up the franchise immediately upon the expiry of his apprenticeship. It is probable that Bowes or his agents had early seen Scott's business-like habits and pitched upon him as one of the fitters of his coal.

" The Bowes estates comprehended extensive coal fields near the Tyne, and whilst these were in process of excavation, Scott was employed to '*fit*' their produce—a technical term, it will be recollected, for transporting coal up and down the Tyne in barges, and negociating its sale. Whether or not (proceeds Dr. Surtees), the fitter is answerable to his principals for the performance of the engagements which he has negociated, depends upon the conditions under which he is employed, and, of course, influences the terms of remuneration. I am not aware upon what conditions Mr. Scott gave his services to the Bowes family :"— he proceeds—" but in 1761, Eleanor Mary Bowes, the heiress of Gibside, became Countess of Strathmore by her marriage with John Lyon, the ninth earl that had borne that title. Upon these foundations, it has been unhesitatingly asserted, in one of the lives of Lord Eldon, preceding that by Mr. Twiss, that ' the father was originally in the situation of a domestic in the family of the Earl of Strathmore."

Thus we find the sacred stream of truth scarcely less polluted by the malignity than by the complacency of biographers !" [m]

In concluding this portion of our memoir, we may remark that Scott appears to have been held in the highest estimation by Bowes, not only in his official capacity, but in being honoured with the particular friendship and confidence of that distinguished person.

Besides his merchandize of coal, Scott appears to have dealt in those necessary appliances, timber, waggon-wheels, and rails for colliery purposes. His correspondents in this branch of trade were various merchants in London, Hampshire, Sussex, and Yorkshire; places where the wood abounded whereof the waggon-wheels were made. They appear to have been shipped to Newcastle by his various correspondents in such immense quantities as to induce us to think the parties believed there was no limit to the demand, and to have doubted the tenor of the frequent and irritable letters sent them by the consignee praying a cessation of the vexatious import in terms, we would be inclined to think, quite unmistakable.

[m] Surtees' Sketch, 46.

His business talent appears to have been characterized by great decision and clearness of action :—he writes the following, 15 Nov., 1745.—" I was duly favoured with y^r sons letter of the 16th last as also yo^{rs} of the 9th inst from Lond$_o$. I was surprised to find by yor sons that a bill sho^d be drawn on me for £140. @ 28 days date and equally surprised you sho^d desire mee to pay it, seeing I am already several hundred pounds out on acco^t of yor goods wch you cannot but be a judge off, when I tell you I have not rec^d a farthing for any you have sent this y^r, and am not in cash for some of other years : as to the people that takes your goods desiring so much credit is only w^t I've often told you in the course of that trade, and if one wont serve them another will, and for any ptical mans part he may chuse whether to deal wth them or not. You desire your acco^t agst Christmas, and I intend it you ; and whose side the balance appears due, let him draw for it. I wrote Mr. Reed that I will take upon me to pay the bill in the spring of the year, if that proposal please, you hear no more of it, but if not, I cannot at this time help it."

In another letter, dated 12 March 1747 (alluding to a disputed account which he desires to refer on the one part, to the man's own relations, and on his own, to their correspondent, Aubone Surtees"), he writes " I am with yours of the 3^d instant and cannot conceive for what reason you sho^d deny my offer of the 26th past, surely you may trust your own relations to settle with me, and it is not more inconvenient for you to send your papers to the north, as its for one to send any to the south, nor have I any friend at London that I co^d trouble without some expence, your relations in the north wo^d take the trouble of giving me a meeting here without putting you to any expence, then why sho^d you deny sending to them. If ever I send so far as London to you, it shall be to oblige you to pay the ballance of your account mention'd in mine the 12th past—being £4. 5s. 3d. If you have any thing to set against it, send it here, and Ill be willing to settle with any body duly authoriz'd by you."

On the 15th of the ensuing month he again writes ; " Capt. Robinson arriv'd here some time since, and as I co^d not take your goods for the reasons given you, he left them to the care of his fitter, Mr. John Robinson^o of this place of wch I tho^t proper to acquaint

---

ª Aubone Surtees of Newcastle, merchant and alderman. He was the third son of Edward Surtees of Woodhead, in the parish of Ovingham, co. Northd., and Frances, daur. and co-heir of William Aubone, esq. merchant and alderman of Newcastle, who was the son of Thomas Aubone of Newcastle, master and mariner. Aubone Surtees was baptized at Ovingham, 4 Sep. 1711, died 30 Sep. 1800, and was buried at the place of his baptism.

º There were two John Robinsons, hostmen at the same time, and for the sake of distinction they were termed *senior* and *junior*. We

you with, so as you may write to Mr. Robinson or some else to take better care of your goods wch at present are lying disorderly on the Key. I am sorry I cannot be serviceable to you any further on this occasion."

On Sunday 21 Dec. 1746, he was suddenly attacked by a severe fever attended with rheumatism. By the 18th of Jan. he was in a way of recovery, but very weak and quite unable to attend to his business, which he did not resume until the middle of the ensuing month as the rheumatism in his hands prevented him from writing. Meanwhile his extensive mercantile correspondence and business generally was effectively carried on by Philip Dunn,[p] his apprentice.

are inclined to think the second is the John Robinson of the text.

John Robinson, *sen.*, the son of Michael Robinson of Blaydon, co. Dur. gentleman, was apprenticed to sir Edward Blackett, bart. for seven years, on 15 Oct. 1694, and admitted to his freedom on 4 Feb. 1701, paying seven shillings to the poor. Nicholas Errington the beadle, having through age become unable any longer to warn the company to meetings, Robinson was appointed to assist him. Another beadle occurs after 1726. The *junior* John, was the son of Thomas Robinson of Worsell, co. York, and apprenticed to Edward Colville, 5 Jan. 1705-6, but on 13 Feb. in the same year, he was by consent set over to Thomas Allan the younger. Colville and Allan were relatives—Lyonell Allan, a merchant of Rotterdam, having married Colville's eldest daughter, one of whose younger sisters (Camilla Colville) became countess of Tankerville. John Robinson remained with Allan up to the taking of his freedom on 23 June, 1713. He had a son Salkeld Robinson, who also became a hostman.—*(Hostmen.)*

[p] Philip Dunn was the son of James Dunn of North Blyth, co. Northd. master and mariner, and apprenticed to William Scott, 2 Jan. 1740. In 1780, Philip occurs residing at North Blyth, and voting at the election of members of Parliament for Newcastle, in

By the latter end of February he was still weak and
unable to go abroad. March 13, he longs for warm
weather to go out, and on the 17th writes " I am yet
so weak I cannot get down staires to any business :"
the middle of the year however, found him bathing at
Tynemouth,⁹ by which time he was entirely recovered.
In a letter to Claudius Heron of London, 25 Octr.
1747, he writes " wee have had the small pox in my
famely wch prov'd fatil to my little daughter Jenny

right of his freedom of that town.   He voted a plumper for Sir Matthew White Ridley, bart., the other candidates being Andrew Robinson Bowes, and Thomas Delaval, esqs.—*(Hostmens' and Poll books.)*

    ⁹ We have not been able to discover when Tynemouth first be-
came a fashionable bathing-place, though it is probable that the
numberless objects of interest it exhibits—its accessibleness, and its
fitness for the purpose to which it is devoted, had not escaped the
observation of the health and pleasure seeking throng in many preceding years.   In 1734, some verses were written by G. K. entitled
" La Belle Assemblée ; or the Tynemouth Bathers, a poem, inscribed
to the ladies of Newcastle, &c.," which under the figure of nineteen
or twenty of the famed Newcastle beauties of the day bathing together at Tynemouth, celebrates their charms in very respectable
verse.   The device is, of course, sufficiently apparent, but it serves
to exhibit Tynemouth even then to have been a place of great resort.

> " Hail happy Tinmouth ! where the Graces sport—
> Where play the Loves, and Venus keeps her court ;
> While from her parent Sea's abundant store,
> Swells in the rolling flood against the shore.
> As flows the am'rous tide, the fair attend.
> Down to the beach the blooming train descend ;
> The billows gently their fair bosoms lave,
> The panting breast repels the circling wave.
>
> •   •   •   •
>
> No more shall Scarborough vaunt her shining Belles,
> Here native beauty all her pomp excels :
> No more shall Bath without a rival reign,
> Our scenes as blooming, and as fair our train.
> To Tinmouth while the Northern Fair resort,
> St. James's boasts not of a brighter court!"

aged 5 years, whom I hope is in happyness, and the twins escaped with their lives very unexpectedly. Tarr water did one of them great service. My wifes had a sore time of it again and is desireing to be duly remembered to you." He mentions a vessel belonging to Newcastle, called the ' William and Barbara' this, it is not improbable, was his property and named in honour of the "twins" In Sept. 1746 he mentions "brother [Stephen] Disbrough" who appears to be a ship captain, and sister Disbrough and al-friends at Scarb^{ro}"—probably his wife, who may have been a sister of our hostman. In like manner in the succeeding year he mentions "brother Glover" elsewhere written "Captain John Glover." Scott was churchwarden of All Saints in 1732. Wednesday, 6 Nov. 1776, "died, in an advanced age, Mr. Scott, many years an eminent fitter in this town."^r Twiss says, aged 79, he having been born in 1696 or 1697. He was buried in the church of All Saints, and in after years a mural monument was erected to his memory by his son, Lord Eldon, in the church of S. Nicholas—mural records of this class not being permitted on the walls of the new church of All Saints.'

^r Newcastle Journal.

' Before passing on to our extracts, we will append a few notes which could not well be introduced in the preceding pages. Charles Montague, of Denton, writing from London. 3 Feb. 1698-9, to his re-

We will at once proceed with the letters, the earliest of which are quite uninteresting as *entire* documents :—

Extracts.

27 Sep. 1745. " The news wee have from Scotland grows worss, its expected the young pretender is now at Glasgow wth 6000 men.

1 Oct. " Wee are ⌊in⌉ such terror of a visit from the Pretender. He and his army now at Edenburg, that I have not time to add."—also to another—

lative, George Baker of Sherburn, says, with his usual spice of offensive caution, (for he suspected everybody of over-reaching him, while over-reaching others)—" I doe insist to have Scott's loading at 8s. 7d. etc., neat." This passage we do not doubt relates to the father of the hostman. *Qu.* Was his (the hostman's) mother living and residing in Sandgate at least so late as 1758 ? as on 21 Oct. that year, the Wallers, Bricklayers, and Plasterers, who had brick and lime works, occur supplying " Mrs. Scott, Sandgate," with a quantity of both of these materials.

HENRY ATKINSON, one of the masters, and afterwards a coal agent of George Bowes, and the father of William Scott the hostman's second wife, was the son of Henry Atkinson, of Gateshead, who in 1685 is styled yeoman, and in 1693 gentleman. He was apprenticed to John Rogers, hostman, from 11 Nov., 1685, and admitted 7 Feb. 1693. His brother, William Atkinson, was also apprenticed to Rogers for eight years, on 8 Feb. 1693, and admitted on 18 Nov. 1702. Henry, son of Henry Atkinson II., was admitted to the freedom of the company on 20 Oct. 1740, which Henry's son Ralph, was admitted 11 Jan. 1771, and died 16 May, 1827.

JOHN SIMPSON, another of Bowes' coal agents, was the son of John Simpson, of Caldwell, co. Ebor., yeoman, and apprenticed to Charles Matfen, hostman, for seven years, from 5 June, 1697. On 24 Sep.

" As wee are dayly expecting the Young Pretender and his army to come here, wee continue in great
terror and confusion, am therefore in hast."—to
another—

"·Wee have been under gr‘ terror and confusion
daily expecting the Young Pretender and his army,
and are still under the same gloomy expectations, and
amidst the great hurry and confusion we have &c."
and " Sh⁴ Huntris come with y‘ goods shall be oblig'd
to land them at Shields, till things settle here in
town. Mr. Silvertop is not yet comd from London nor
I suppose will not (as he's a Papist) so long as these

in the same year, he was set over to Robert Taylor, and on 19 May,
1699, (his master being dead) to Phillis Taylor, the widow. His
admission to the fraternity took place on 15th Nov. 1704. His son
John Simpson was sheriff in 1733, mayor in 1742, and governor
of the hostmen's company, from 5 Sep. 1745 to his death in 1786. He
was a man of great wealth and liberality, and on 4 Jan. 1758, expressed his readiness to contribute 100l. towards the obtaining of an
act of parliament for preventing shipmasters taking their freight of
coals over-sea, when they had cleared for the coast. At the court
held 4 Jan. 1761, " our worthy governour most generously made a
present of one hundred pounds to the fraternity to defray the necessary expences thereof, and for such intents and purposes as they
shall see fit and convenient." Simpson lived in the Broad-chare,
just north of the great gate of the Trinity-house. His son
John Simpson married Ann, daughter of Thomas, earl of Strathmore, by whom he had Maria-Susanna, the late lady Ravensworth.
WILLIAM SELBY, who is mentioned as being employed as one of
the coal-agents upon his good behaviour, was the son of William
Selby (described as late of Beal, co. Northd. gentleman, deceased)
and apprenticed to John Armorer, hostman, for seven years, from
1 March, 1715, but on 15 June following, set over to Francis Armorer. He was admitted to the freedom of his fraternity on 6 May,
1723.—(Waller's and Hostmen's books—Surtees, &c.)

times last., If Capt. Barrow come I shall be obliged
to land your rails below the town, for there is no
such thing as bringing them to this confus'd place."

8 Oct. "Some advices from Edinburgh this morn-
ing brings acco^t the Rebels are moving tow^{ds} us w^{ch}
occasions me to conclude."

18 Oct. "Heres a great many wheels comd from
your parts, amongst them are y^m p Huntris and
Tristram, it wo^d been well you and your neighbours
had sent us as many guns in their place wch wo^d been
a far more desireable comodity, as the rebels stil lurk
ab^t Edinburg and often threaten to give us a visit,
but we shall soon be in a capacity to defend our
town."

22 Oct. "We have of late been under great ter-
rours from the near approch of the Pretender's Son
and his army, but now as wee have got most of
our forces here, are by them made easy."

29 Oct. "We have now a great army in town
and ab^t us wch raises our spirits, yet we are not wthout
our fears from the Rebels, who are strongly incampt

, This would in all probability be George Silvertop, against whom
complaint was made 20 Nov. 1749 for exercising the trade of a hostman, not being a free burgess of Newcastle, or of the fraternity of
hostmen. A committee was thereupon formed to consider the affair
and see what methods should be taken to restrain him. No result
is recorded.—(*Hostmen's books.*) Scott occurs selling him some
waggon rails in Ap. 1745.

at Dalkieth and are putting themselves in a fighting posture."

15 Nov. "The Rebels has given us very great uneasiness, for before his Magestyes armys came here wee were daily afraid of a visit from them, they are now investing the city of Carlisle 45 miles west of this place wch city wee have reason to be afraid will be obliged to surrender to them if the forces wee have here don't go very soon to their assistance, and wee sho^d be sorry they sho^d go for fear the rebels sho^d pass them and come here."

18 Nov. "His magesties armys marchd to Hexham with intention to assist [against] the Rebels but it proved too late, the rebels have got possession of that place and his magesties army are returnd here again, and this day our churches, houses, glass houses, maltings &c. are filled with them. I know not when wee shall get any time to do business again, for believe me wee have and have had very troublesome times. I wish you may not know or experience the like. Its said the rebels intend to place a governor at Carlisle and leave some men there and march to Lancashire, if so his magesties armys will follow them."

22 Nov. "Since I wrote you last wee have had great alarms from the Rebels and had his magesties armies gone any sooner from hence than last Satur-

day wee have great reason to believe they wo^d have comd to this town instead of going to the city of Carlisle ab, 50 miles west of this place wch city and castle they took this day week, by wch doubtless theyl strengthen themselves. His magesties army under com^d of Field Marshall Wade who marched last Saturday to the assistance of Carlisle, returns here to-day again to guard this town wch wee are but too sensible the rebels are desireous to have. Youre happily cleare of such troubles and may it long continue so, and wee freed from our present troubles for wee have had such times of it as scarce any business can be minded."

26 Nov. "His magesties forces that was here, began march this morning by way of Durham in pursuit of the rebels who its said are got into Lancashire, with wch please to acq^t my f^{rds} at Scarb. Archb^d Stewart esq. prov^t of Edinb° took post for London on Sunday mo. last."

29 Nov. "The Saltish sloop of warr came here yesterday, and bro: certain acco^t of 10 sail of French ships having landed men in Scotland, wch make us now think the rebels will return back to joyn them, but God grant they may be disappointed."

3 Dec. "Wee had a great army here who left this place some days ago and are gone in pursuit of the rebels now in Lanchashire. They or Gen. Le-

goniers army will wee hope meet with and defeat, but sho^d it happen otherwise and the rebels sho^d return to Scotland no doubt our armies will also return this way wch wo^d be the occasion of an advance of wheat and flower."

27 Dec. "Our time is greatly taken up by this rebellion; the rebels have got into Scotland again, except some part of them that is in Carlisle Castle which place our noble duke has envested and resolv'd to have it out of their hands."

10. Jan. 1745-6. The rebellion affairs put most people here about of[f] business for more than 2 or 3 months but as the rebels are drove back into Scotland wee are now under no apprehensions of their ever returning except to receive their punishment."

31 Jan. "The wheels made up of the peices you sent here are yet unsold, the prices runs very low at psent occasioned by too many wheels being imported last year, the dealers mostly have 6 or 9 months stock by them at this place, and you may judge by the following advertism^t how full Sunderland is. Jan^ry 25. To be sold at Sunderl^d a fresh parcel of birch wheels and beech rails and plank at the lowest prices, enquire of Mr. Thos. Smith who will shew the same. Who these wheels &c. belongs too, I know not, but the advertism^t standing in our newspaper make the dealers here expect wheels and rails for almost

nothing. If I had your wheels sold, shall make up your acco^t for last year, as yet have received very little on acco^t of your goods so am a great deal afore-hand with you. There has been no such thing for some months past as getting any business done, people has been so much taken up by these rebellious affairs wch we tho^t had been almost over, when the rebels was drove into Scotland, but all of a suden we were amais'd with a battle wch happen'd between them and our forces, but now as his Royal Highness the Duke of Cumberland has got into Scotland, wee hope to have such acco^t of the reb^s soon, as will be pleasing to all his magesties faithfull subjects, and see trade go forw^d again in peace and quietness. I am wishing you much prosperity this new year, and many ensuing."

18 Feb. "Wheels are at present a great drug from so many y^t came last year. Rails will be want-ed but the people pays so badly for them that wo^d weary any body to serve them, a years credit is no-thing with them. I shall endeavour to send you a loading or two of coals as the ships are begining to trade. Bark runs from £3. to £3. 10s. p tun just as its in goodness, the last you sent was but indifferent and not lik'd."

28 Feb. "You say you have bo^t a peel of rails you formerly wrote ab^t, if you mean ash rails theyl

come too late, for the gentleman that wanted them is already servd. Your timber is not yet arr^d. I find the best oake rails will scarcely give 6d. p yd this year, as there will be a great many cut in this countrey and led to the wag^n ways at 6d. p yard. This pcell of rails provd very indifferent and were badly squard."

To Mr. Richardson, Gt. Ayton, co. York, tanner :
· 23 March. " I have spoke to several masters to load for you, but coals bearing so great a price at Lond° as from 36s. to 38s. p cha. I cannot get a ship but on extravigant terms, one mas^r asked me £100. for the run, that is to load here and load back for you, and carr^d only 4½ keels. Glass bottles are now double the usual price on acco^t of the duty to be laid on them by act of parliament. If you wo^d have any sent, youl let me hear again from you, for shall miss no opportunity to send yow a ship load of coals when I meet with a master that will take a reason· able freight."

12 Ap. 1746. " We were made very joyfull yesterday with the news of the Hazard sloop and rich cargo being taken in Scotland wch wee hope will distress the rebels."

18 April. " The prices of grdstones continue according to advice given you Feb. 8 1744-5, viz. 1, 2, 3, 4, 5, 6, 7 at 18s. p cha. and 8 foots 58 inches high

E

the same and every grdstone above 58 inches high 1s.
p inch more price for every inch exceeding 58 inches
in height, and the merch^t giving orders for grindstones to pay the custom house charges &c. 11d. p
cha. as also mas^{rs} fre^t and run the risque of the seas
&c. and pay for them p bills 2 months after shipping;
but if north country stones will do for you I mean
such as you sometimes bo^t of one Mr. Barber, co^d
serve you on lower terms, but not any otherwise for
this river stones such as I've always sent you.—What
some mas^{rs} told you ab^t burning papists chapels is too
true there has been too much of it, from the mob
thinking the people of that profession encouragd the
rebellion."*

13 May. " Your favour of the second ins^t came
early to hand last post, in answer youl have acco^t below answerable to your request. I am sorry any one
of the grindstones sent you by mas^r Moss sho^d prove
contrary to your expectation, they went all good from
me on bord the ship and the money is due on ship-

---

* This alludes to the burning of the mansion and private chapel
of the Riddells, in Gateshead, on the arrival of Duke William on
his way to Culloden. The outrage was effected at one A.M. on the
morning of 28 Jan. 1745-6. At the same, or a somewhat later
hour, certain disorderly persons broke into a portion of the ancient
nunnery of S. Bartholemew in Newcastle, where had been erected
another Catholic chapel, and took away and destroyed several goods
belonging to it. The corporation liberally offered 50l. for the dis-
covery of the offenders.

ping them, tho dont think much of giving a month
or two credit when requested, and charge attending is
always p^d by the buyer as any of yor f^rds here can tell
you. I scorn to charge you otherwise than I do
every body else and tho I sho^d be glad to serve you I
sho^d not desire your favours but when I serve you
as well as any person here. As to flagg stones, I
don't deal in them but you may be well served by one
Mr Thos Peirson stone cutter of this place. When
ever I have any call for cheese or corn shall acquaint
you."

27 May—*to Mr. Richard Chitty, Singleton, n^r
Medhurst, Sussex.* "Its true by chance I sold some
of Mr. Midford's rails at 5½d. p yard but the greatest part of them are yet unsold and find I shall be
oblig'd to take 5d. p yard if not less for them, for
several percels are com'd since from Northampton &c.
and none of them sold, I therefore cannot advise you
to send any rails, nor will w^gn wheels fetch any price
to your expectation. If ten tun of good bark come
here soon it will fetch £3. 5s. or £3. 10s., or at Berwick £4. p tun. I shall send you 3 or 4 kitts of
salmon p the first ship I can get to come to you w^th
coals, in the mean time sho^d be highly pleas'd to see
you at Ncastle."

8 June—*to Messrs. Dover and Wolff, Lyndhurst,
New Forrest.* "I fancy the dealers in w^n wheels

will expect to have wheels soon 'em given, if such great numbers continue coming. I dont see but the dealers may expect them at least at very low rates, those of yours I expect to get sold this week at or about 7s. a wheel; your rails are very ordinary. When I shall get 'em sold or at what prices cannot yet say, as the river is as full of them as of wheels."

18 July—*to Mr. West, Slyndon, n'' Arundel, Sussex.*—"The best w^n wheels will now scarce give 5s. a wheel and some part of yours are very bad, and here is a great many wheels here, and the dealers also so full that they have not room for any wheels, that many of the wheels already here will either be sold for very little or go to decay."

24 July—*to Mr. Richd Chitty, Singleton, Medhurst, Sussex.* 'The Ark of Scarbro:' Mr. John Masterman arriv'd here last Sunday and bro^t me (without any advice from you) about 20 load of rails and 185 waggon wheels, wch rails and wheels are both greatly decayed. I wont say but the rails may some time pay the fr^t but the wheels will contribute very little towards it, for I fear they never will sell at any rate but for firewood, considering the great numbers of wheels that are here unsold and many of them fresh. I am perswaded it wont be worth any bodys while to send any here for some years."

25 July—*to Mr. West, Slyndon, Arundel, Sussex,*

" At this rate of hurrying goods here, some will be
sufferers, and no time given me to settle with people
here and abroad, and when goods comes at this rate
the dealers think they do me a great piece of service
only to take them, and in short I should have a mint
of money to answer draught freights."

6 Feb. 1746-7. On the old grievance, his apprentice, during his master's sickness, writes to Mr. West,
"My master is surprised you sho^d have any such notion
as that he can sel wag^n wheels for ready money, as you
bid him sel yours in the yard now, at a time when the
the dealers are full stocked for a year to come, some
of them having no less than 7 or 800 aforehand. My
master has forc'd of some of yo^{rs} this week but what
he's to have for them or when he's to be paid he
knows not. He has had so much trouble about
these, and for all he can do he cannot get them all
sold, make him wish he may not see a wheel come
here this year. The 60 old wheels you sent in July
last will never sell at all."

20 Mch.—*to Davis and Wollf, Lyndhurst, New
Forest.* " I cannot understand what you and your
neighbours means by sending so many waggon wheels
here, some will be great sufferers thereby, nay I may
say you all will be sufferers for theres none can sell
any wheels at present, the dealers are all so full
stockt they have not room for any more and I have

told you so over and over again and must desire now that you'l send no more to me without advise. P.S. If you send any more wheels to me without advise as above you'l excuse me for taking charge of them."

27 Mch. 1747—*to Daniel West, Slyndon, n^r Arundel, Sussex.* " You surprise me to hear you have shipp'd some wheel pieces on bord Mr. Masterman and that you intend to send 500 wheels here this year wch I cannot think you'l be so imprudent to do after my advising you so often to the contrary ; but sho^d you do so I wo^d not pay your loss by them for £50., nor shall I be willing to take charge of them for there is scarce room about the town for them already here, and the key is fill'd up with them. No less than about 2000 com'd within these 14 days from Lyndhurst consign'd to different people."

8 May—*to Mr. Martin Conwenberg.* " I have shipt on bord the John and Fra', Capt Geo. Muriss, sixty chald^{rs} of gr^dstones agreeable to your orders and hope youl receive them soon, to yor content, and make no doubt of your'e sending remittance for the same in good time. I should think it a favour you wo^d buy me a peice of Holland cloth to make shirts for myself about two guilders a yard or ell, two po^d of green and two po^d of boea tea, and a gallon of cinoman water of the best sort, wch may charge me with in your acco^t."

26 May—*to Constable, Newsham, and West.*
" Being now resolv'd to receive no more goods such as
w^n wheels, rails, and such like from any body, finding
I no sooner receive them, than soon after, the money
is expected, tho I can make it appear I often don't
receive the money for them in less than sometimes 12
18, nay for some 2 years and upwards, so am now de-
termin'd to employ myself in making up accounts wth
such people as I have dealt with that way and
amongst the rest yours wch I propose to send in July ;
in the mean shall not pay any more bills, but shall be
ready to pay you whatever may appear due to you,
not doubting if on a fair account you may be found
in my debt, you'l do the same by me."

5 June—to "*Mr. Claudius Heron, at Mr. Nich.
Brooke's, peruke maker in Little Argyle Street, near
Swallow Street, Argyle Buildings, London.*" " I think
to let alone the chaires, but desire you'l take the
trouble to buy me two lottery tickets and regester
them in some office that will advise me when they
are drawn and w^t they come up, and for the charge
shall be accountable to you. Mr. Fenwick, Parker,
and Rutter, are out of town this week, but shall en-

---

* Christopher Rutter, hostman, succeeded to the freedom of that
fraternity by patrimony from his father Christopher Rutter, baker
and brewer, (the son of Lancelot Rutter) who by having been apprenticed to James Barker, baker and brewer, on 30 Dec. 1709, and
obtained his freedom of the same by due service, became entitled to

deav' to see them next week and give you their answers ab' your bills on them. Bartho. Henzell[w] will go
or send to Durh[m] next, week and expects will get that
affair ab' the hh[d] of cyder that went to Ald. Wharton clear'd up, and will after his return, write you himself. He's been wth the labourer, who well remembers
he d[d] it to the carrier and will swear so. Mrs.
Lamb is yet alive and is likely to live a while longer.
My spouse joynes &c."

13 July—to *Mr. Claudius Heron.* "I rece[d] of
Mrs. Thorp £2. 3s. 6d. and money for all the bills
you sent me, excepting that on Mr. Fenwick who

the franchise of the hostmen in virtue of the charter of James the
First,—an arrangement whereby those who wished to invest the profits of a successful occupation in some other business than that whereby they had amassed them, were enabled to become coal-owners
in whole or in part, and while accumulating still further riches
through the "sable ore," were not in any way exciting the envy or
diminishing the custom of their less fortunate compeers in the company to which they had really served an apprenticeship. Christopher II. had a numerous issue—his son Jacob Rutter, an eminent
brewer, born 15 Oct. 1733, was admitted of the Bakers and Brewers,
4 Oct. 1755, was churchwarden of S. Andrew's in 1756, and buried
29 Ap. 1759. His widow Elizabeth, remarried John Graham,
(afterwards John Graham Clarke) 3 Dec. 1762, who was the father
of the present James Graham Clarke, esquire. Christopher was
buried 28 June 1755. His elder brother (like his own son)
was Jacob Rutter,—admitted to the hostmen by patrimony, 4 Jan.
1719, elected sheriff of Newcastle, 19 Sep. 1720, died 28, but. 30
May 1722. His widow remarried 8 Jan. 1722-3, John Ord, Attor-
ney-at-law.—*(Hostmens', and Bakers and Brewers' books; Reg. S.
Andw. &c.)*

[w] Of one of the interesting families who introduced the manufacture of glass to the banks of the Tyne. Bartholemew Henzell

promises to pay it soon but am afraid he won't. I shall in a week's time send you a bill to answer the lottery ticketts. The cyder you have in B. Henzells celler is dead and sour, may be made vinecar by puting a busell of gooseberrys into [it], shall wee try."

14 Aug.—*to Mr. Cl. Heron.* " Since mine of the 13th past have not been favourd wth any of yours. I have been oblig'd to go often to Tinmo : for the benifit of bathing, else sho^d have sent you the inclosed bill ere now, wch is for £28. 5s. 8d. on Mr. Thos. Dean wth a bill of percels of grindstones. The last bill I drew on this gentleman was long of paying, on

was a wine cooper, and lived in the Broad-chare, on the Quay-side, so called in contradistinction to the rest of the chares, this being the only one of the number which will admit of the passage of a cart between the kerb-stones. He was apprenticed to William Brown, junior, cooper, on 26 Sep. 1711, and admitted to freedom on 19 May, 1719. He had issue, Isaac, John, Charles, and Peter ; and two daughters, one of whom married —— Baker, a viewer at or near Tanfield, and the other, a counsellor living in Gottenburg, on whose death she espoused Joshua Henzell, a half-cousin. Bartholemew, who died before 5 May, 1755, was the son of Isaac Henzell, who at his son's apprenticeship in 1711, is described as "late of Newcastle, gentleman, deceased." His position in society as a glass-manufacturer would even in our day, give him an easy title to this style, but at his own period there was a something in his family which seemed to claim it as a species of recognized right, beyond the award of mere courtesy. It is remarkable that in the reign of Elizabeth, when Thomas and Balthazar Hennzes, *esquires,* make their agreement to set up glassmaking in England, they designate themselves as we have indicated, and stipulate for the aid of three assistants whom they style *gentlemen.* Something of the same sort is observable throughout the parochial registers of the town, particularly in that of All Saints, where there is an al-

F

wch account am afraid you'l have some trouble in get-
ing this money, therefor must beg your pardon for
putting this task on you, but hope you'l do what you
can in procuring the money, as I shall do for you wth
Mr. Fenwick who still puts of your bill on him for
£5. 17s. 10½d., and it is but small hopes I have of
getting it before his mayoralty be over that is Mi-
chaelmas.   I fancy you have not yet bought the lot-
tery tickets else sho^d have heard from you, but sho^d
your silence be for want of health, I sho^d be very sorry
to hear it.   I wish you well.   P. S. have inclos'd l^r
of advice for Mr. Dean, please put a wafer in it before you give him it."

most invariable distinction made in favour of the family of Henzell.

On 11 Dec. 1674, this Isaac Henzell writes "to Mr. Wm. Aubone
present in Sandgait" [by the way here we find a good proof of what
we have elsewhere advanced—for here is William Aubone, esquire,
alderman, and father-in-law of Lord Eldon's father-in-law, *living in
Sandgate*]—Sir, My love to y^u sir, I having severall somes of money
to pay this weak on bills and fright for [goods] hath put me to a
strait to pay my servants [this] weake, now my desire to y^u is y^u
will [please] to lend mee six pounds and send it by the bearer Elizabeth Swalloe, and if y^t please to take glas for it, y^t shall have
it when this I owe y^t is paid, or if not glas, I will pay y^u again in
mony, a fortnight after Christmas, so hopeing y^t will doe me this
kindnes, I rest yor friend Isaac Henzell."   Below, the document
bears evidence of the successful termination of the request, (how
should it be otherwise, upon such fair terms?) Elizabeth Swallow
placing her mark as the testimony of having received the six
pounds "of Wm. Aubone by order and for account of Mr. Isaac
Henzell and for his doughter Margaret Henzell, to pay again
uppon demand."—(*Coopers' books., Lansd. MSS., Church Regs., Rob-
son papers.*)

21 Aug.—*to Mr. Martin Convœnberg.* "I am greatly surprised and concerned to hear you complain of the grindstones sent you p cap^t Geo. Muris [who] told me you were highly pleasd with them wch gave me great pleasure, and Thos Dawson, who is now sitting by me protests he never shipt a better percel, and is willing to make affidavit there was no such things as holes or pits in them stopt up with earth; however in regard to what you say, and rather than you sho^d be disoblig'd, wo^d be willing to allow you 20 of the 40 guilders you say you lost in your profit of these stones, and if I do so, than might have sold them better of my key. Theres no body can serve you better wth grindstones 62 inches high, than I can do; the prices of such size on your key will be 21 guilders each."

29 Aug.—*to Wm. Mitford, esq.* "The coal trade having been so bad here this year, that the dealers who had yor former goods have not been able to pay yet, but as the trade begins to mend, I expect to get some money of them soon."

20 Oct.—*to Mr. West.* "It may not be amiss to inform you some people begin to want wag^n wheels, tho some others have too maney, and here is 500 or 600 yet unsold, tho I've none to sel, and my friends Mr. Shafto and Mrs. Bell begin to own they want, and there will be beach rails wanted." And to

Davis and Woollf, he writes. " The sooner 10 or 15 load of more plank comes the sale wo^d be made more certain, for in the spring there will be of it coming from other parts and better wood. About 100 wagon wheels of large sizes wo^d not come amiss now.

25 Oct.—*to Cl. Heron.* " I duly rece^d your favour of the 3^d inst. and was in hopes I sho^d before now had to acquaint you Mr. Fenwick had paid your bill from many fair promises he's made me, notwithstanding wch I despair of getting the money by any fair means, I sho^d rather say civil means, so you had better write him you must take other methods than you have done if he does not pay the money, for believe me I have so often spoke to him myself, and sent to him, that I am quite asham'd of speaking to him any more, for whenever I speak to him myself he bids me send my servant along to the Mayor's House at such a time and he'll pay the money, and when my servant goes he tells him hele see me and pay me the money, and so puts me off from time to time, both wth respect to yor money and some I want of him myself. I doubt yo're the same way serv'd with Dean, having not heard from you [that] you have rece^d for my bill on him, wch if you have not, I desire you'l take such methods as you may gett the money of him. I observed you had bought me two lott. ticketts at £10 each for wch give you credit and may if you please send

them to me by your next. I went to Gibside on Friday and ret^d yesterday. Most people there ask'd after you, and I presented your service as you desir'd. I was sitting by the esquire and his good lady when your letter came wth some pictures wch seemed kindly received. Mr. Colpitts was there and told me you had wrote him to pay me four guineas, but he had sent you that sum befor he rece^d your letter. I am glad your journey to Winchester &c. was so entertaining to you, and wish you all the pleasure you wish in this world.

27 October.—*to Claudius Heron.* "What is wrote you before, I intended you last post, but wanting a frank I delay'd it to come p this post, I have told you I was at Gibside but tho^t not of franks till I came to close for you. I have your favour of the 22^d wth your bill on Geo. Baker, esq., for £16. 10s. wch shall some way endeavour to get of him. Mr. Leaton is to be here to-day, and I expect a frank of him to cover this, and as soon as I can get more shall send you some. I am glad you have got Dean's money, and this morning I spoke to the mayor, but no better, I shall expect a few lines from you to give him. Was that hhd of cyder you have wth Henzel, mine, I wo^d take any thing for it I co^d get, a small matter is better than nothing, besides it will be to remove, the cellar being let."

30 Nov.—*to Mr. Cl. Heron.* " I sent yor lre. to our mayor who, as before, pro^d to pay yor bill soon, and I have sent again, but get no money yet. This day I have sent on bord the Duke W^m of Sund^ld, 4 doz. of the best must^d [48℔ of superfine flowers of mustard, @ 16s., £3. 4s.] in a box directed agreeable to yo ord^n. P.S. I have had Mr. Burfield a distiller, to taste yor cyder, who says its not worth a farthing for any use whatever."

28 Dec.—*to Cl. Heron.* " I duly rec^d yor favours p Mrs. Green's. Theres nothing can be said for bad luck. I intend you my blanks soon, in the mean time when you get abroad you'l let me know w^t you think they'l give. I am afraid you'l have often to write to Mr. Fenwick and Mr. Baker befor you get yor money. As to the former I know not how to come by what I want of him myself, he still puts me of (as he does many others) with fair promises of paying me yor money and mine too; but when I shall get either of them, I know no more of than the first day the debts were contracted; and as to the latter, I wrote to him and he sent me for answ^r p Mr. Antho. Dunn that he wo^d send the money ag^st the bill became due, and I have sent sever^l times to him since, by Mr. Dun, who is frequently writing to him ab^t business, but no money has com'd yet. I wish I co^d be servisable to you ab^t the cyder, but every body

that tastes it, says its good for nothing. I thank you for the news you send, and wish his majesty good success. Wee are like to have gr^t wars in Northumberl^d betw. Ld Ouslouton and Mr. Allgood occasioned by the death of Mr. Fenwick of Bywell. My poor wife is like to catch a fever but desires to be duly remember'd to you and Mrs. Green. Wishing all happiness to attend you both, &c."

8 Jan. 1747-8.—*to Richard Chitty.* "Beach rails will not be wanted as formerly. I mean not so many, the long wag^n ways being on the decrease."

15 Jan.—*to Cl. Heron.* "I am with your favour of the 9th instant and am glad to hear of your'e better health. I sent to Mr. Fenwick the morning I rece^d yours, and rece^d for answer he wo^d see me soon, and I've heard nothing from Mr. Baker. I think of sending my servant to his house next week. I observe you rece^d the mustard and hope it gives content. Youl reoeive inclosed my lottery ticketts, youl please let me know when you sell them, and for what. Mr. Leaton[*] teld me yesterday the Ledstone family were

---

[*] William Leaton was apprenticed to Charles Atkinson, hostman, on 23 Dec. 1721, and when admitted to the freedom of the company on 26 July, 1733, made the usual, but optional grant of five shillings to the poor. Under the style of William Leaton of Gibside, co. Dur. gentleman, on 16 May, 1759, he became the mortgagee of premises in Grindon chare and in other parts of Newcastle, for 600*l.* Under Feb. 8, 1792, there is mention of Anthony Leaton of Whickham, co. Dur. nephew, residuary legatee, and sole executor named

all well, and that he tho[t] they wo[d] be going to London soon. My spouse is bravely recover'd and desires her compliments to you and Mrs. Green."

19 Jan.—*to Mr. West.* "Sailor wages runs high, and freights sho[d] do the same. I hope your'e pretty easy of your fingers. My spouse was taken very ill on Christmas day, but is now pretty well again. Our service to Mrs. West."

6 March—*to Cl. Heron.* "You'l think long to hear from me, and all I've to tell you is that I sent my servant to Mr. Baker's the week before the Alnwick Election began, and he staid there from morning to night, but Mr. Baker came not home, so he left a mem[dm] of his business, and desired Mr. Baker wo[d] send the money for your bill, w[ch] is not com'd yet; and I spoke to Mr. Fenwick last Thursday, and he promis'd me faithfully he wo[d] send me the money for

in the last will and testament of the said William, as also under 9 Oct. 1779, there is mention of Anthony Leaton of Tantoby, co. Dur. yeoman, cousin of William Leaton, deceased, by whom the mortgaged property was disposed of.

On 22 June, 1724, George Bowes writes from London to Mr. Thomas Maynard "I have waited with impatience these three or four last posts in hopes to have received a letter from Mr. Rudd, but to no purpose. Therefore I must beg of you once more to call upon him to give you an account upon what lands my mother's rent charge is settled. I desire you and Mr. Leaton will break open my study and drawers at Gibside and see if there be any writings there that is requisite to be sent to town for the satisfaction of my mistress' councell, and afterwards put new locks upon the doors and give the keys to sister Betty. You and Mr. Rudd may consult what is proper to be sent; I think they will insist upon your bill in 2 or 3 days, but I see none of it yet. I believe at last I must return you both bills but shall wait your answer. I've had a letter from Mr. Colpitts, and he says if his friend has not already paid you the money due from him, hele pay me it. Mr. Leaton told me yesterday he beleiv'd the Ledstone family wo^d set out for London very soon. During the election Mr. Baker was at Alnwick, and was in Northumberland for some time before."

13 Mch.—*to John Oviatt.* "I am with your favour of the 4th instant advising of 182 wheels and 1214 feet of rails you have consigned to me in the Good Intent, Capt. Jno Robinson, tho not arriv'd yet, when he does, am sorry I cannot serve you in selling these goods for am already engag'd in more wheels and rails than I can or have any prospect to sel this year, the markett is so full ; therefor you'l please to think of

a copy of my father's and brother Thomas' will and my ladie's marriage settlements together with the writings belonging to the two estates, Streatlam and the Highlands, upon which her jointure is to be. I believe that Streatlam and Highland writings are al that can, so have sent sister Betty y keys and have desired her to go along with you to help you to find them. I desire yeu will hasten up these writings as soon as possible and send them by William Leaton who may come by the stage-coach, for till I receive them in town, I cannot set forward for the north. But if yea and Mr. Rudd think proper to send up more writings belonging to the other estates, I desire you may. I shall write to you next post and direct to Streatlam, when perhaps I shall be able to send you further directions. If you hasten up these writings, I hope I shall be with you at Gibside in less than three weeks time."—*(Hostmen's bks.—Sanderson Deeds—Sharp MSS.)*

some other person to receive yours from the captain
when he comes, the wind being at north east it may
be some time ere he arrive. This port is really so full
of goods of this sort, that I cannot think of engaging
with yours, as know not how to give you any satisfaction in the sale of them, whoever sells them must sub-
mit to low prices and long credit."

18 Mch.—*to Cl. Heron.* " I rece'd yours of the
12ᵗʰ instant and on the 16ᵗʰ Mr. Baker sent his servant with £16. 10s. for your bill. Mr. Fenwick
shall not want sollicitation. I shall try what I can
do with him again, and again. Mr. Colpitts I hear,
is at Ledstones, and Mr. Leaton tells me you'l certainly see that good family at London soon.ʸ You
tell me I know not what, about the Northumberland
election, pray tell me what you hear about Mr. All-
goods petition, surely justice will be done him; is a
sheriff to strike out votes, if so, sheriffs only are to
chuse members for parliament, and not freeholders,
nor freemen such as dear sʳ. &c."

15 April 1748—*to Willm. Staite.* " I have ask'd for
a tun of steel for you but the gentlemen of the foun-
dery say they cannot tell when they can let me have
such a quantity, they having so much bespoke by
their friends at London, who as they say can take

ʸ George Bowes and his family—the allusion about Brook-street
a few lines after will also probably relate to them.

all they can make. I see the letter that came from London pretending you boasted you co^d be serv'd at Newcastle wth steel, at a time you co^d not have it at London, wch was soon after mine to you the first of the year, and the gentlemen here tho^t it wo^a disoblige their friends at London to supply you. I cannot remember the names of the persons that wrote, but probably it might be the person you say told you co^d be serv'd wth steel here."

26 April—*to Cl. Heron.* "I am very sorry to hear your great complaints, and heartily wish you better health. I have been sore frightened with the rheumatism and have not been clear of the gravel a long time, but live in hopes the warm weather, when it come, will relieve me. I am glad to hear the good family in Brook street are all well, long may they continue so. The box you mention for Mr. Collpitts is not yet com'd when it does, shall forward it to Streatlam.* Mr. Fenwick has not yet paid your bill nor have I any hopes he ever will, without you take some other methods, tho he desires I'll keep it another week, and promises fair, but I am confident it will be to no purpose, for he pays no body any thing without trouble. If he does not pay your bill by this day week, [I will] send it to you."

* Bowes was of Streatlam, as well as of Gibside.

10 May—*to Claudius Heron.* " I have kept your bill longer than I said I wo^d in mine of the 26th past on his faithful promise he wo^d this day pay it, but find its to no purpose my keeping it any longer, therefor have inclos'd it. I dare say you'l believe I've us'd my utmost endeavours to got the money but its scarce possible to get any money from him but in the way I have befor teld you. I hope to hear from you soon, and of your better health, and whenever I can serve you in any thing here, you may always freely command, &c. P.S. The indorsment that was on the bill was to my serv^t who has been times out of number demanding the money."

The Oppressed Man's Outcry: the Sufferings of John Hedworth.

REPRINTED BY M. A. RICHARDSON,
IN GREY STREET, NEWCASTLE.
MDCCCXLVII.

ONLY 100 COPIES PRINTED.

The history of the sufferings and privations
of John Hedworth of Harraton posses-
ses great local interest, and although the
declaration of a suffering man must be
received with due caution, yet he appears
to have had just grounds of complaint against
the authorities of the Commonwealth.
The original tract is preserved in the valuable collection of John Moore, esq. of Bishopwear-
mouth; and we are indebted to sir
Cuthbert Sharp for the illus-
trative notes.

M. A. R. at Newcastle
this August,
mdcccxlvij.

MAJOR JEREMIAH TOLHURST who occupies so prominent a position in this doleful relation of Hedworth's sufferings, was a free burgess of Newcastle, and having obtained, as we have stated, the lease of some colliery property, sought the power of fitting his own coals, which he was unable to effect without the permission of the company. On 28 Sep. 1655 he petitions the fraternity of Hostmen for this purpose, and though the charter granted them in 1600 required absolute *residence* within the liberties of the town to constitute a claim to the freedom of the company, " nevertheless the court [having] vsed vpon extraordinarie and speciall causes and occasions to admitt some persons of eminence and qualitie to their freedome"—and " takinge into due consideracon the qualitie of the said Jeremie Tollhurst being gouernour of the towne and garrison of Carlisle and a gentleman willinge and able to be vsefull and serviceable to this towne and companie"—thought fit to admit him to his personal freedom for the term of his natural life, disenabling him from making apprentices free, and from transmitting the freedom to his wife should " she ouer liue him." Tolhurst proved himself both " willing and able to be vsefull and serviceable " as his brethren the Hostmen had calculated, and he occurs resorting to London with others, to defend their interests there in a consultation with the privy council of the Protector, and on other occasions doing them good service.

Hostmen's Books.

The Oppreſſed Mans Out-cry:

O R .

An Epiſtle writ by John Headworth *of* Harraton *in the County of* Durham *Eſquire,*
the 11 *of* September 1651. *Vnto the Honourable Sir* Henry Vane *the Elder, a Member of the Honourable Parliament of the
Common wealth of* England; William Vane
his ſonne; Lieutenant Collonell Paul Hob-
ſon, John Middleton, *Eſquires, and Members of the Committee of Militia, in the
County of* Durham, *by Authority of Parliament.*

Honourable and worthy Gentlemen.

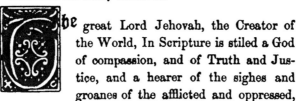

Þe great Lord Jehovah, the Creator of
the World, In Scripture is stiled a God
of compassion, and of Truth and Justice, and a hearer of the sighes and
groanes of the afflicted and oppressed,
who in Scripture hath fully declared himself to be
an angry and severe Judge, and punisher of Tyrants
and Oppressours; yea and of those that shut their
Eares and harden their hearts against the mournfull, pittifull, and just complaints of the afflicted
and distressed; and he by his speciall Providence
hath put Power, Authority, and Magistracy into

your hands, being Members of that Committee, that
have the chiefest command in this County, under the
Parliament (the Supreame) at your beck; and therefore by him in Scripture are stiled gods upon earth;
and in that regard you ought to be like him, not
onely in tender compassion and mercy; but also in
truth and justice; and hearers of the sighes groans,
and mournfull lamentations of the afflicted and oppressed. In the serious consideration of which give
me leave to cry unto you, and acquaint you, That I
am the Son and Heire of a Deceased Knight, Sir
John Hedworth; who was Lord, Owner, or Proprie-

---

* The oppressed man was the son and heir of Sir John Hedworth of Harraton, knight, the head of a rich and antient family.
Sir John was of an easy and careless disposition, unsuited to the
troublous times in which he lived, and his son suffered the penalty
of his indolence.

The collieries having been leased to Sir William Wray, a papist
and recusant, were sequestered and leased under the State to George
Grey of Southwick, and the Lilburns. Sir Arthur Hesilrigg, governor of Newcastle, and (Lord of the ascendant) seems to have set
both law and justice at defiance, turned out the Lilburns, and let the
lands and collieries to Col. Hacker, Col. Mayers, and Major Tolhurst. In the midst of his troubles, John the "oppressed man"
died in 1655, and his widow Susan, daughter of George Grey of
Southwick, married John Jackson in the following year, 14 July,
1656, who was knighted by Charles II., 22 May, 1660 "as a present mark of his Royal favour for his loyal services and sufferings
in the Wars."—*(Parliamentary Intelligencer, p. 565.)*

Thomas, the father of Sir John Jackson had purchased from Sir

tor of the lands of *Harratton* in the County of *Durham*, and all the Cole-mynes thereof, or thereunto
belonging; and left them unto me by an Ancient and
unblemished Intayle, as strong as the Law of *England*
(my undoubted Birthright) could make any, as his
Eldest Sonne and Heire; and being by his decease left
young in years, and destitute of the support of Pow-
erfull Friends and Allies and thereby fit.to become a
Prey to every devouring Wolfe, or greedy great
Man; that should have a covetous eye to that Inheritance, that my forefathers strongly and Legally in-
tayled upon my father and my self; and it was my
unhappy fate to live in the Age, wherein Sir *Arthur
Haslerigge* became Governour of *Newcastle*, a man of
an high and covetous spirit, the whole County of

John Hedworth several detached portions of the Harraton estates,
and Chatershaugh descended to the family of Peareth by intermar-
riage with one of the grand daughters of Sir John Jackson.

The oppressed man gives a grievous detail of his sufferings from
the tyranny of the unscrupulous Governor, Sir Arthur Haslerigg.

The family however, revived in better times, and regained a con-
siderable portion of their estates: and the two grand daughters of
John the "oppressed," Dorothy and Elizabeth, married respectively
Ralph Lambton of Lambton, and Sir William Williamson of Monk-
Wearmouth. The name of Hedworth is still preserved in both
families. The portion of Williamson was purchased by Lambton,
and the antient family residence of the Hedworths, called Harraton
Hall, is now the seat of the Earl of Durham, under the name of
Lambton Castle.

B

Durham being (as by his constant actions he declares)
too little in Revenue to satisfie, or content his greedy
appetite, and a man thàt will admit of no rule to
walk by, but his own crooked and perverse will of
Sword; who casting a more then an *Ahabs* eye, upon
my poor Vineyard at *Harratton*, abhorred to be so
righteous unto me, as wicked *Ahab* desired and profered to be to poor *Naboth*, who proferred him for his
Vineyard the worth of it in money, or a better for it.
But Sir *Arthur Haslerigge* finding my Lands and Coale-
mines at *Harratton* were profitable and pleasant, and
lay commodious for him to adde to his newly com'd
by great estate; yet though he were inferiour in
Power to *Ahab* a King, would be more unrighteous in
practise to me, then he was to poor *Naboth*, and
therefore would take from me my Collieries and
Lands, yea, and my Cattell too, and that without so
much as ever profering me as good for them in exchange, or the worth of them in money; or so much
as one penny for them in consideration; yea, or that
so much as ever setting up and Legelly producing the
least shadow or pretence of Title against me, more
then his will, pleasure and sword; yea, and to agra-
vate his covetousnesse and tyranny exercised to the
height against me he would not onely take my Inheritance, Goods and Cattell from me for nothing, by
his will, but he would doe it in such a way, as that I

should be left destitute for ever hereafter, of all hopes
of friends to recover it, and therefore he would totally destroy and crush to pieces, not onely in estate,
but also in good name (which to an honest man
ought to be more pretious then much sweet oynt-
ment) my Father in Law Master *George Grey*,[b] and
my old friend Master *George Lilburne* thereby for
ever hoping to deterre any man of Power or Interest,
in the least to medle with me, to help to ease and
redresse me; and all this done unto me at such a
time, when the Righteous and just God is abroad in
the world, in Power and Majesty, to destroy Kings
and Princes, and the greatest of their followers : for
tyranny, injustice and oppression ; yea, and at such
a time when the Parliament of *England*, his Masters,
have rased and maintained a bloody and costly
warre, declaredly to defend the Liberties and Properties of the People ; yea, and at such a time when
they themselves execute severe justice for secret
transgressions done in holes and corners upon their
own members : Witnesse my Lord *Howards* bribery.

[b] The Greys of Southwick descended from Henry, Lord Grey
of Codnore. George Grey, father in law of Sir John Jackson, purchased *Hedworth's lands* in Southwick; his son George Grey,
was a Captain of Foot in the Army of the Parliament, and his
brothers Richard and Ralph were living in · 1651. In the fourth
descent from George, the heiress of Grey of Southwick intermarried
with Sir Charles Grey, grandfather of the present Earl Grey.

And that Sir *Arthur Haslerigge* hath oppressed me, and taken from me and my Tenants my Estate, is evident :

1 First as to my Cole-mines, the profits of which he and his under Commissioners, in their Certificate, Printed in Lieutenant Collonell *John Lilburnes*[c] Letter to foure of the Commissioners at Haberdashershall, dated the 30. of *July* 1651. page 11. line the 3. and 4. hath valued at fifteen pounds a day in clear profit, which by the Yeare at that rate, reckoning 365. dayes to the Yeare, amounts to full 5475. pound *per Annum*, and yet they then sold the Coles for eleven shillings the Chalder ; and these now sell them for thirteen shillings the Chalders ; the high injustice and tyranny in his taking away of which and still with a high and strong hand as unjustly detayning of it, is so fully set out and proved by authentick Records, in the fore-mentioned Printed Epistle, (especially in my Tenant Master *Iosiah Primates* Petition to the Parliament, delivered at their door in Print to their Members upon the 22 of *July*

---

[c] John Lilburn was a Lt. Col. of Dragoons in the service of the Parliament ; but a troublesome servant to his employers,—of independent memory. He was tried for high treason in 1649, and after many years of opposition to all authority "free born John" died a Quaker and was buried at Moorfields in 1656. His brother Robert was some time Governor of Newcastle, and was also one of the Regicides.

1651. And recorded there, page 16, 17, 18, 19, 20)
that *I* need say no more of it, but referre you to the
said Epistle, one of which *I* make bold herewith
hnmbly to. present unto you all, for your serious and
carefull perusall.

2 Secondly, he and his under Commissioners hath
as arbitrarily and tyrannically taken away from me
almost 300 pound *per Annum*, of my Land of Inheritance at *Harratton*, and have let both Colliery and
Land to Collonell *Hacker*, Lieutenant Collonell
Mayers, Major *Tolhurst*, or other of his Officers and
souldiers ; of which Land *I* was (being neither Papist nor Delinquent) in Legall and quiet possession
for about three years together, before they pretended
to sequester it from me ; and although *I* had an Order dated the 12 of *July* 1650. recorded in the 29
page of the aforesaid Epistle, that requires, That in
case *I* was in actuall Possession at the time of the
Sequestring my said Land and were no Papist nor
Delinquent ; that then *I* should be restored by the
Commissioners of Parliament to the possession taken
from me, giving security to be responsible for the
Profits of the Estate, in case it should not prove
mine ; And although there was never any pretence
of my being either a Papist, or Delinquency laid unto
my charge ; and although I have fully proved, by the
Oaths of authentick Witnesses *viz.* master *Iohn*

Clifton of *Gateshead*, and Master *Thomas Petty* of
Durham, recorded in the said Epistle, page 28.
That I was in quiet and peaceable possession of the
said Lands, at the time when they were sequestred,
yet will Sir *Arthur* not suffer the Commissioners of
Sequestration of *Durham*, to obey the said Order,
or doe me any manner of justice or right; but in
stead thereof, hath commanded one of them, *viz.*
Collonell *Francis Wren*[d] to goe to the Judges of Assizes, and command them from him, to suffer me to
have no benefit, nor Priviledge of the law of *England*,
my Grand and undoubted Inheritance and Birthright.

3 Thirdly, Sir *Arthur Haslerigge* and his said under Commissioners, who are wholly at his beck and
command, and dare doe nothing against his will and
directions, have most illegally, arbitrarily, and tyrannically robbed and taken from me almost sixty Head
of my Cattell, some of which were well worth seven
or eight pound a piece, I having been bid for ten
Oxen then of that number seven pound a piece, ready
money; and six more of them were Stots; for some
of which I was bid five pound a piece, and these they
took from me being my own proper goods, and no

[d] Francis Wren of Henknoll, co. Durham, who espoused the
cause of the Parliament from conviction, and who excercised the
duties of his office of sequestrator with great moderation.

mans else in the world neither directly or indirectly. And my absolute propriety in them, I have fully proved by Legal testimony, Copies of which depositions are recorded in the aforesaid Epistle *pag*, 33, 34, 35. the height of whose injustice to me in the two last perticulars of my Land and Cattell, I cannot to your Honours better set forth then is already don in my Printed Petition, delivered to the Parliament, upon *Iuly* 23 1651, and recorded in the foresaid Epistle, *p* 31, 32, 33. to which I humbly refer you; all which Cattell I value at 300l.

Its true they pretended they were my Father *Greys*, which if they were, (as in the least they were not at that time, nor any one of them for almost 12 moneths before) yet he is neither Papist nor Delinquent; but is and hath bin a zealous, active wellaffected Parliamenteer; and a Committee man for divers years together, unspotted and unblemished; as is very well known to you all four. But further, they say my Father *Grey* ought one *Iohn Iackson* a Delinquent money, who had not payd his Composition, whats that to me; but fullier to answer that *I* say, my Father *Grey* avers he owes him never a penny, nor never bought, nor sold with him in his life, for twopence; nor never took no Land of him, nor Cole-pits, nor no such like things; but its true, he confesseth he took Land of his Brother *William*

Iackson, who had a Legal right to let it, for the payment of his Portion, and his Sisters, who had a Decree in Chancery in 1639, to authorise him so to doe; and also had the Order of the Committee of the County of *Durham* to enable him so to doe, which Order was procured and obtained, by the speciall desire, and Petition of the wife of the said *Iohn Iackson*, when his Land was under Sequestration; and yet for all this hath the said Sir *Arthur Haslerigge* and his obedient creatures, by his will and pleasure, taken the said Land from the said *William Iackson* (who was neither Papist nor Delinquent) and his Sisters, and conferred it upon the said Delinquent *Iohn Iackson*, who had no present right to it, by means of which those of them that yet are alive, are ready to famish and starve through poverty and want.

But may it please your Honours, admit the said Cattell that *I* aver was mine had been my Father *Greys*; and admit the said *Iohn Iackson* the Delinquent, had pretended my Father had ought him mony, yet upon what ground of reason or Law had the Commissioners at *Durham* to beleeve the said *Iackson* a Delinquents bare averment, before my Father in Laws, who is no Delinquent, but every way an honest man: but *I* further answer, *Iohn Iackson* the Delinquent had compounded, and actually got off his Sequestration, about a yeare before the taking away

my Cattle, and in that regard was in a sense in *statua
quo ;* and if any man ought him money, his just and
regular way was to goe to Law for it, and there re·
covert it, as other English people doe; and not for
Sir *Arthur* and his Commissioners to be their own
Carvers, to make that a pretence to ruine and destroy
those who they had a desire so to doe unto, under
pretence that they ought a Compounding Delinquent
money; which if they did yet had Sir *Arthur* and
his Commissioners (neither by Law nor Ordinance)
any power at all, to drive their goods, halfe starve
them, and then sell them, at most for halfe the price
of their first worth, and doe with the money what
they pleased, as with me in my present case they did ;
nay although the said *Iohn Iackson* had not payd in
all his Composition, yet neither by Law nor Ordinance they had no power to sease and sell the Goods
of those that really ought him money, much lesse of
those that he only pretended ought him money; much
lesse could they sease and sell the Goods of those
that he never pretended ought him a penny, which is
my case; for their regular and Legall course in case
of his wilfull, or negligent non payment of his fine,
had been to have re-sequestred his Lands again.
But this high piece of injustice as well to my Father
Grey, as my selfe he assures me, he will particularly
and fully annotomise in Print; and therefore to him

c

I now leave this, and all his other, and many oppressions and wrongs by Sir *Arthur Haslerigge*, which I beleeve the world will shortly see in Print by him, in their colours.

4 Fourthly, I beseech you observe here is to me out of my Colliery lost 40s. a Week, and 10*l.* at Christmas, and 10*l.* at Easter for two years amounts to 248*l.* besides lost out of my Land, at 300*l. per Annum*, or thereabouts, for one year and three quarters of a year, comes to 525*l.* Lost by my said Cattell 300*l.* All three of which put together comes to 1703*l.* besides in severall Postings, and other Journies to *London*, charges staying there, Fees to Lawyers and Solliciters, with Clarks Fees for Orders, &c. Charges for Witnesses, severall times to *London* and *Durham*, and many other incident charges depending upon my almost two years troubles, above 300*l.* For I am sure of it, one Journey to *London*, and charges there, cost me above threescore pounds, besides the losse of my time for the said almost two years, and improvement of my Stock and Land, with the deniall of me the benefit of the Law, and thereby with other ingredients, the losse unto me of many opportunities I have had to regain and possesse severall large parcels of mine Inheritance at *Sunderland*, and severall other places, and making me poor and low, forcing me to run into debt, with disgracing my reputation

and credit; yea, and to adde to all this, by his bury-
ing me alive (as it were) if I had not by Gods good-
nesse found unexpected, extraordinary, choice, cor-
dial and faithfull friends; by which means I am really
damnified, I am confident of it, at least 5000l. besides
the foresaid 1703l. or thereabouts, that I have lost
by Sir *Arthurs* matchlesse and unparalel'd cruelty and
tyranny. Over and above which, If my Colliery be
worth that rate of 15l. a day, That Sir *Arthur* and
his Commissioners in their foresaid Certificat values it
at; my Tenents, Master *Primate*, Master *George
Lilburne*, and my Brother Master *George Grey* Junior, are damnified by their almost two years losse of
it about ten thousand nine hundred and fifty pounds;
of all which cruelty and injustice exercised towards
me, and upon me Collonell *Francis Hacker* (now a
Collonell of Horse in the Army under his Excellency,
the victorious Lord Generall *Cromwell*) hath been no
small instrument and principall Agent to execute upon
me arbitrarily and illegally; sending his souldiers, or
Troopers, with severe commands to handle me ruffely,
without pitty or compassion, when by their will and
swords they took my own from me; threatning them,
That if they did not execute his tyrannicall and unjust commands effectually upon me, he would Cashiere
them out of his Troop and Regiment as some of them
selves have confessed, and all this he did, as is evident,

to make himselfe rich and great with my Colliery and
Lands, of which Sir *Arthurs* darling the said Collonell
Francis Hacker, must become the chiefest Farmer,
which, in the conclusion it may be, may have as
sharp sauce following it, as *Naboths* Vineyard had to,
or for *Ahab*; which if it have, I hope Sir *Arthurs*
Lieutenant Collonell *Mayers*, and his busie and late
upstart Major *Tolhurst*, with his pedling Lieutenant
Braine the insolentest fellow of all the rest, will not
goe scot-free; Thus most noble Gentlemen, have I
most truly, though briefly layd open my wounds unto
you, for which as yet in this our English *Gilead*, I
can find no Balme, although I have left no just and
ordinary meanes unassayed, that is possible for the wit
of man to attempt ; as

1 First at the beginning, I and my relations at the
Committee of *Durham* did what in us lay to preserve
our rights, but Sir *Arthurs* will, long sword, threts,
and bended fist, was too hard there for all our Law,
Right and Reason. And then, when by his will and
power, my right was carried from me there, *I*

2 Secondly, appealed to the chiefe Commissioners
above at *London*, and there *I* freely spent my money
amongst the Lawyers and Solicitors, to gaine the best
advice *I* could thereby, but my businesse going on
very heavily; *I*, at last, found out two faithfull
Counsellors, *viz.* Lieutenant Collonell *John Lilburne*,

and Major *John Wildman*; upon whose faithfulnesse, understanding and valour, I cast all my said affaires : and they played the part of honest, and faithfull men for me ; and had many a sharp and bitter tugg with Sir *Arthur*, and the Commissioners above as you may partly and truely Reade in the foresaid Epistle of Lieutenant Collonell *John Lilburnes*, which yet is far short of what I my selfe heard expressed there, and when I was wearied, tyred and almost spent with charges, and delayes, and could get no manner of Justice from their hands ; *I*

3 Thirdly, followed the advice of one of them, *viz.* Lieutenant Collonell *John Lilburne*, and Petitioned the Parliament, and had his personall and zealous countenance in it ; but they being full of weighty businesse (for so at most *I* must but say) had no time to Reade my Petition, although *I* stayd at *London* so long, till *I* was fain to Ride Post to come down, to the expected Assizes at *Durham ;* and at my departure, *I* principally left the care of my businesse with my said faithfull friend Lieutenant Collonell *Lilburne ;* who it seems being in some dispaire of getting my Petition at Present read ; and he as to me appears, judging long delays to be my ruine ; in the

4 Fourth place, he hazarded himselfe ; amongst other things he had occasion to Publish, to Print my oppressions, and cruell sufferings in that foremention-

ed Epistle of his, to foure of the Commissioners at
Haberdashers-hall, to which he sets his hand three
times; And although Sir *Arthur Haslerigge* at *Durham* the other day (as the said Lieutenant Collonell
informes me) would have had some people to beleeve,
he durst not, or would not own it; And therefore desired his Brother *Gore* to deliver a Message from him
to the Lieutenant Collonell; which was, That if he
were a Gentleman, he desired him to own the late
Book called his, and to send him one; which being
delivered to the Lieutenant Collonell, by his Brother
Gore; he desired him to tell Sir *Arthur*, That if he
were a Gentleman, he intreated him to be an instrument, that they both might appear face to face, at
the Bar of the Parliament, and he would engage
himselfe to him, to own so much of it (as he was confident) should make his very heart to ake; for as the
Lieutenant Collonell saith to me, the Book or Epistle
contains in it a high Charge against Sir *Arthur
Haslerigge*; and by the Law of *England*, and the
practise of the Parliament it selfe, in the Earle of
Stratfords case, he saith, it is at his own choice, which
piece of it he will begin with, to make good against Sir
Arthur first, and not to be prescribed by him, or any
else for him, to begin with, what in it they please;
and *I* my selfe am sure of it, the main and principall
part of it, he hath there sufficiently proved by

authentique Records, which to my great cost and
expences *I* my selfe know to be too true; but besides, Sir *Arthur* needs not in the least to be affraid
of the Lieutenant Collonells not owning the Book, for
I my selfe, with many more, hath heard him often
doe it; and he hath told me, that (as I remember)
the very day he came out of *London*, he went to the
Honourable the Speaker or the Parliament, for his
Post Warrant, and told him to this effect, That he
he had a Book at the Presse, which would be finished
and Printed within a few houres, against Sir *Arthur*
Haslerigge, for his oppressions to his Unkle, Master
George Lilburne, my selfe, and severall others of his
relations; and therefore intreated his Honour, in
case that in his absence that Book, by reason of the
high language in it, came to be questioned in the
Parliament, that he would be pleased to oblige him
so far to him, as to acquaint the house that it was
his, and he would justifie it with his life; and therefore humbly besought him to intreat the House to
punish no body for Writing, Printing, or Dispersing
of it; but to lay the whole load of it upon himselfe;
and if he pleased, in case the House were angry at
the Lieutenant Collonell for it, he intreated the
Speaker to send him but two lines by the meanest
Messenger in the World and he Ingaged to him to
leave all his businesse in the North and to come Post,

to the House, and justifie the truth of the said Book
with his life : and further told the Speaker, That
seeing in ordinary wayes he and his friends could get
no justice against Sir *Arthur*, he intended to goe to
the Generall to *Scotland*, and as Sir *Arthur* was a
Member of the Army, being a Collonell of a Regiment, and Governour of a Garrison, under the Gene-
ralls Power; he was resolved at a Councell of Warre,
to Article againt him; and he was confident they
would heare him, and doe him right : the first part
of which, he told me he acquainted the Lord *Grey* of
Grooby with : and earnestly begged of him, in case
the said Book was questioned at the Councell of
State, that he would answer for him, as he had intreated the Speaker to doe in the Parliament : And
he furthur told me, That before he took Horse at
London, he went to Haberdashers hall and gave and
caused his Books to be given away, in the very face
of the Commissioners there, and their Officers ; and
that when he took his Journey he brought many of
the said Books along with him ; and at all, or most
places where he came, gave away the said Books with
his own hands, as his own ; and having but one left
at *York*, at the Postmasters there, Master *Pierson*,
Sir *Arthur Hasleriggs* Clarke, or Secretary, came into
his Roome, about twelve a Clock at Night, and he
pulled one of the said Books out of his pocket, and

to Master *Piersons* face owned it, for his; and Read
him some of the smartest Passages in it, and told
him, he had but one, of many of them left, or else he
would have given it him, to give to Sir *Arthur Haslerigge ;* but being he had but one, he was resolved to
keep it till the Morning, and give it to his noble and
honoured friend, Master *Luke Robinson,* the Parliament man, and did so ; and intreated him seriously
to Reade it all over; and, as his Book to shew it (if
he pleased) to Barron *Thorpe,* then in person at his
Inn : And also he further told me, That at his comming into the County of *Durham,* he waited upon the
Generall at his Quarters at *Branspeth,* on purpose
about it ; having left order at *London,* to send severall of them to the Generall, and the chiefe Officers
of the Army into *Scotland,* which arrived safe in their
hands at *Scotland ;* but the Generall being very busie,
and ready to March from *Branspeth,* he could have
no time to speak with him about it ; but inquired
after it of some of his principall Officers; who told
him the Generall had seen it, and as they thought,
had Read it, for as much as there was some discourse
betwixt him, and some of the officers about it ; some
in the Army apprehending the things layd to Sir
Arthurs charge, to be very foule and base, prest that
there might be a hearing of it at a Councell of
Warre, which was promised, after the great busi-

nesse was over; at which tidings, the Lieutenant
Collonell was very glad, and Ingaged upon his life to
make the said Book good; and when he had done
(having got a new recruit) he gave some of them
away, as his Books, upon the very place, to some of
the Officers of the Army, and yet for all this, the
Lieutenant Collonell tells me, since his comming from
London (his Letters tell him) he was Posted up Publiquely (as he beleeves by some of Sir *Arthurs* Agents,
on purpose to disgrace him) for running away, for
Printing the said Book, which he durst not own; and
that if any man would bring him in, he should have
700l. for his pains; and by others, as he beleeves,
of the same Agents, he was publiquely in *London*
Posted up, for riding away to the King of *Scotland*,
with 500 Horse; and if any could bring him in, they
were profered 500l. for their paines.

But fully understanding, by the said Lieutenant
Collonell, how my Businesse was above, and how little
hopes there was to get any speedy remedy there;
and fearing that the length of time of getting a hearing in the Army would be too long for my pressing
necessities to stay; they having in a manner taken
all that ever I have in the World from me, and allow me not one penny to live on out of my Estate, so
that if I had not some true friends to help me, I, my
Wife, and small Children (for any thing they afford

me) might either starve or bog ; besides they suffer my Houses to be so, that they are ready to fall down upon the ground ; and force me to hire my own ground of them to put in some Cowes to give a little Milke, to feed my poor young Babes.

And my Mother, and her Daughters are in the like case, they having not, for almost two years, received from them 30l. to buy them bread, although my Mothers Title hath been the chiefest that sometimes they have set up to Sequester the most of it, upon pretence of her Recusancy ; and therefore whether she have a Title or not, yet they Sequestring it upon that pretence, they ought by the Law of *England* to allow her the thirds out of it ; but they are like greedy Cormorants, that will swallow all ; I say considering, and weighing all my necessities, and pondering in my own selfe, and taking Counsell what I had best to doe, I did in the

5 Fift place, upon the 23 of *August* 1651, with some friends, goe to *James Liddell*, their steward, and demand of him the immediate payment of some Rent reserved to me upon the Colliery ; the which he absolutely refusing to pay, I made a formall re-entry upon my Colliery, as by Law I might ; upon which a company of men came violently upon me, that called themselves souldiers, and act upon my Ground like savage Bares and Wolves, or

theeves and robbers, and will produce unto me no written Order or Warrant, to give me a rationall ground, to judge from whence they come, or who they are: upon which, I the second day of this *September* 1651, repayred to *Durham*, to the Commissioners sitting there, and they disclaime them, and avow they know nothing of them, till told them; but yet would grant me no Warrant to take them away, onely they promised me to speak with Major *Tolhurst* about them, who it seems is their Commander, as well as his souldiers; whereupon the next day I writ a Letter to the Constable at *Harratton*, and others of my neighbours, charging them at their perils, upon my Ground to harbour them no more, nor joyn with them any longer to robbe and steale from me my Coles by force and violence; and that they might all take notice of their own danger, I caused the said Letter to be Printed and delivered to them severall Copies, of which, I make bold herewith to present unto you for your serious perusall: but divers of my said neighbours persisting still in their evill dealing with me, I have sent to *London* for processe for every one of them that are tardy, as well Keel-men, as others, and doubt not of a sufficient remedy at Law against them all, without interuption from the Committee of indempnity; where yet *I* should not be sorry to be brought into, being apt to think *I* shall not fully get my complaints heard.against Sir *Arthur*, till he or some of his Agents be forced by me to turn complainants: but Processe being in my own understanding, to short weapons to reach souldiers withall: in the

6 Sixt place, upon the fourth of *September* 1651, *I* went to *Gateshead* accompanied with my Father in Law Master *George Grey*, *Richard Lilburne* Esquire, Lieutenant Collonell *John Lilburne* his Sonne, and my Brother Master *Ralph Grey*, on purpose to speak with Sir *Arthur* about these things; but he being busie with the Committees of the Ministry, and so not to be spoken with, we all (saving Lieutenant Collonell *John Lilburne*) went to Major *Tolhurst*, and acquainted him with the substance of all passages at *Harratton*, and demanded of him the said reserved Rent of 40s. *per* week, which he refused to pay, and acknowledged, That by a verball command of his own (which is not worth a button, nor can be no security to the souldiers) he had sent the said souldiers to keep the Possession of the said Colliery: adding he was betrusted by Collonell *Hacker*, and Lieutenant Collonell *Mayers*, and the rest of the Gentlemen that had taken it, to keep it, and he would keep it: so receiving no satisfaction at *Newcastle*, and clearly finding Major *Tolhurst* durst not give to the souldiers a Written Warrant, or Order, to be their security, rule and guide: in the

7 Seventh place, I desired my Father, Master *George Grey*, and some other friends to hasten to *Sunderland*, to disperse my said Letters there; and again to warn all the Keel-men, at their perils to fetch none of my Coles, nor none of the Ship-masters to buy none of them, and my selfe with Lieutenant Collonell *Lilburne* rid away to Master *Timothy Whitinghams* being a Justice of Peace, and Read him the said Printed Letter and fully acquainted him, That a company of rogues, who called themselves souldiers, were come upon my ground, but could produce no Commission from any body that sent them; nor the Commissioners at *Durham*, nor Major *Tolhurst* would not under their hands own them; and they, like bloody rogues, beat, and had almost killed some of the people, who they forced to leade away my Coles to the water side; and some of the said souldiers with their

---

* Whittingham was the great grandson of Dean Whittingham and grandson of Sir Timothy Whittingham, of whom the following strange entry still exists in All Saints Register, Newcastle " Dame Whittingham murthered by hir husbande" bur. 17 April, 1604. Mr. Surtees says very truly that " there are more ways to break a woman's heart than one," and he considers that the expression must be taken *cum grano salis.* Certainly the record however, carries the presumption that the lady was not killed " with kindness." Be that as it may, his grandson Timothy appears very careful not to enter into the meshes of doubtful legality at the request of the oppressed man, but very dexterously shifts the charge to some tangible point wherein he might exercise his magisterial authority.

own hands loaded my Coles into Keeles, and carried
or sent them away, and thereby Feloniously robbed,
and stole from me my real and proper goods; for
which, as he was Justice of Peace, forthwith we desired his Warrant as Fellons, to bring them before
him, which we very much pressed upon him, as his
duty by his Oath, and the Law of *England* to grant;
but he refused, and desired time to consider of it, and
speake with Sir *Arthur* about it: upon which, Lieutenant Collonell *Lilburne* desired him to tell Sir *Arthur* from him, If he, and those under him, were
affraid and ashamed to give the souldiers at *Harratton* under their hands, a written Commission, or
Order to act, and that Master *Whittingham* refused
to grant his Warrant to bring them before him, upon
our complaint; we would not be affraid nor ashamed,
to doe the best we could, to expell force, with a
stronger force: and if any of the pretended souldiers,
were knockt on the head in the scuffell, for any thing
we know, from the Law of *England*, they had their
mends in their own hands: but if he would send his
Written Order for the souldiers Warrant, and let us
Coppy it out, we would not trouble or molest the
Souldiers any more; and so we were content, that he
should take till *Munday* at night to talk with Sir
Arthur about it; and we being both at *Durham* upon *Tuesday* last, being the ninth of this present *Sep-*

tember; Master ̄*Whittinghams* man brought to our Inn a Sealed Letter, the Coppy of which followeth,

For his very good friend Lieutenant Collonell John Lilburne *these,*

Kind sir,

pon *my more serious thoughts, and strickt perusall of the Printed Letter which you left with me upon Fryday last*; *I plainly see a matter of Title, and a* meum *and* tuum *in controversie betwixt the State, now in question, and Master* John Hedworth, *of which thing you well know the Law is the proper Iudge, and can and must decide it*; *and the Civill Magistrate no way concerned in the businesse. Yet Sir, I am so tender and carefull of your safety and my own duty; that if either your selfe, or Master* Hedworth *be afraid of life, or know any man lie in wait to robbe you, or either of you; or if any Fellony be committed, or Robbery done upon your Person or Persons; upon Legall Information, I shall be very ready to serve you, and grant my Warrant: Also if there be any force either by Entry or Deteyner, I shall not in the least be wanting unto you and the publique, to joyne with another in Commission with my selfe, to*

*view, and remove as occasion shall offer: In briefe, this
is all, but that I am,*
Sir, your affectionate friend to serve you,
Timothy Whitingham.
Holmeside the 9, of Sept. 1631.

Now most Honoured Gentlemen, I pray seriously
observe Master *Whitinghams* Letter, who if he had
been a man according to which (God in Scripture)
requires every Magistrate, *viz.* A man of Courage, I
am apt to beleeve he would scarce have Written this
answer to our Legall demand; but I desire to be as
sparing of him as the nature of my businesse will permit me; but yet I beseech you to take notice, That,
I think, the Civill Majestrate is the proper Judge of
the Law and not the souldiers in the least; much
lesse those that onely pretend themselves to be souldiers; and besides, I beseech you observe, That in
the eye of the Law Fellony and Robbery may be as
well committed upon my Goods taken out of my
House, or Ground, as from my immediate and proper
person; and so much we possitively layd unto the
charge of those sturdy rogues, that pretend themselves souldiers, upon my Ground, who have no Formall, nor Legall Commission to authorise them in the
least to doe as they doe; and upon our so serious
laying Fellony to their charge, and offering by the

E

Law to make it good; he ought by the Law, without
any more dispute, to have granted us his Warrant,
at least to have brought them before him, to have
examined them; by means of which, I should either
have knowne some, that judiciously and formally
would have owned them; or have had some evident
demonstration, that they are the men, that Major
Tolhurst by word of mouth sent, or else have had
them clapt in that place, that would have kept them
safe till they were fully fit for the Gallous, their deserved Portion.

But most noble Gentlemen, by all the fore recited
dealing with me you may clearly see, I am made the
most miserablest spectacle, and object, in *England,*
being robbed by Sir *Arthur Haslerigge,* &c. by will
and power, of my Land, Colliery, Goods, and Cattell,
and damed up, that I can have Justice no where, to
obtain a little of my own to buy me bread, to keep
me, my Wife, and young and tender Infants alive;
nay, that which is worst of all, I am expressely by
Sir *Arthur Haslerigge* himselfe, in the presence of
my selfe, and my Brothers, Master *George* and *Richard Grey* and Master *Clifton,* and many others, absolutely commanded to be robbed and deprived (before I had committed any crime) of all the priviledges
of an Englishman, by being debarred to have the
benefit of the Law, against any of those that detain

other parts of my Inheritance from me, then now is
in the possession of the State; in the detension of
which, the State gets no benefit at all. Wherefore,
heare, O Heavens, and give eare, O Earth; and if
any bowells of Compassion, Justice, or Mercy be in
you, pitty, commiserate, and help to relieve me, a
most distressed and cruelly oppressed, young Gentleman, that with grand oppression, and unparallel'd
cruelty, is like to be destroyed by Sir *Arthur Haslerigge*, (when in *England*) at that time when the
Parliament thereof hath many Armies in the field, to
fight for the Laws, Liberties, and Properties of the
People; and therefore as you are men; nay, men of
Honour, Conscience, or common honesty, or as even
you came from the bowels of Women, O help, help,
help me, and my perishing Family, in my transcen-
dant and great distresse, and put forth some of that
Power, betrusted to you by the Parliament of *England*, as you are Members of the chiefest power in
this Country, *viz.* Commanders and disposers of all
the Forces, and Millitia there; and send forth your
Warrant, and Souldiers, to command before you
these theeves and robbers, now upon my Ground,
that call themselves souldiers, and so being within
your Jurisdiction, are under your immediate command, and compell them by your power, either to
produce before you a formall and written Warrant

to justifie them in what they have already done, or
in default thereof to send them to the Goale, as
rogues, theeves, and robbers ; and as one of you is a
Parliament man, and as either the Sperit of Honour,
or an English man dwels in you, send this my complaint to the Parliament, and earnestly intreat them
in my behalfe to Reade my forementioned Petition
depending before them and doe the right against all
the cruell oppressions of their own Member Sir *Arthur Haslerigge*, who is the greatest dishonour uuto
them (by his oppression and tyranny) in all this Nation. And as one other of you hath been a Member
of the Army in a place of eminency there ; and as
either the spirit of a Souldier, or a man of magnan-
imity dwells within you, send this my mornfull complaint, lamentation and out-cry, to his Excellency, the
Lord Generall *Cromwell*, and the Honourable Officers of his Army, and intreat of them in my behalfe,
to take Cognizance of my great oppressions by the
Members of their own Army, *viz.* Sir *Arthur Haslerigge*, his Collonell *Hacker*, his Lieutenant Collonell
Mayers, his Major *Tolhurst*, his Lieutenant *Brume*,
and all the rest of his Officers that have unjustly oppressed me, and helpt to robbe me of my Estate ; And
also, I pray you put him in mind, of the dishonour Sir
Arthur Haslerigge hath done unto him, and the af-
front he hath put upon him, by his turning honest,

firme, and fast men, to him, and the Common wealth, out of places of authority in this County; and his placing in (as Governours thereof) not only newters, but known Delinquents; yea, and particularly, his making Collonell *Francis Wren*, the onely man under him (as it were) to govern and rule the whole Country, after his excellency had Cashiered the said *Wren* in *Scotland*, for his unworthinesse and basenesse : And for your noble favours manifested unto me, in the things desired of you, in this the day of my great distresse and calamity, I shall be very much obliged in the presence of my Friends, whose names as Witnesses are hereunto subscribed, to acknowledge my selfe to be Ingaged to remain,

Gen'l-men, your greatly distressed Friend, and humble servant heartily to serve you and the Commonwealth,

John Hedworth.

From my own House at Harraton the 11, day of September 1651.

Witnesse

George Grey. *Richard Grey.*
John Lilburne. *Ralph Grey.*
Ralph Rooksby.[t] *Roger Harper.*

[t] Ralph Rooksby of Harraton was related to the Hedworths and was the third husband of Susan Grey; mar. 26 Feb. 1678.—*Abbey Register.*

Richard   bp. of Durham

Bishop Barnes's Injunc-
tions to the Clergy of the
Diocese of Durham.

IMPRINTED BY M. A. RICHARDSON,
IN GREY STREET, NEWCASTLE.
MDCCCXLVII.

ONLY 100 COPIES PRINTED.

TO

THE RIGHT REVEREND

EDWARD LORD BISHOP OF DURHAM

THIS IMPRINT OF AN ACT OF ONE OF HIS

PREDECESSORS IN THE SEE

IS INSCRIBED

WITH SENTIMENTS OF PROFOUND RESPECT

BY THE EDITOR

cclesiastical Charges of
a period just posterior to the
Reformation cannot be count-
ed otherwise than valuable, as
illustrating in the most au-
thentic manner, many points
of Ecclesiastic ceremonial
or polity. The Charge is
procured from one of the stray volumes of the
Randall MSS. and we are indebted to
Dr. Besly, vicar of Long Benton,
for our translation of the
earlier portion of the
document.

M.A.R. at Newcastle,
this April,
mdccclvij.

ie Martis viz. primo diem. Octobris aō Dñi 1577 loco consͣ infra Galeleam ecclie catlͤͤis Dunͤ corāͤ Reᵈᵒ in Xͭo pr̄e 7 dnō dnē Richardo dͥa pvidentia Dunͤ Epͦo suam sacram scͭam Sinodum in totum clerum dioceseos sue Dunelemeñ p̄dict celebrante, in p̄sentia mei. Chr. Chaitor nōry puᶜⁱ &c.

Quibus die 7 loco dcūs Reͤᵈᵘˢ pr̄ post finitam concionem more solito mandavit totum clerum p̄d̄em p̄conizari quo po²conizat, idem Reᵈᵘˢ pr̄ pt. exhortaꝯnem suam paternā ōīb3 clicis interessentibus factam dedit et ministravit quasdam suas monicoñes et injūctiones sinodales in Ᵽgameno scriptas quas mihi Crōfero Chaitoʳ notario pu^{oo} : ᵱdict pr̄ ꝓlegendas tradidit, quarum quidem̄ monicoūm 7 injꝰctionum sic plectar. iꝺm̄ Re^{dus} pr decrevit copias magr̄o Robto Swifte viċio suo in spūalib3 gñali 7 archñis tam Duꝝ quam Northumbrie, necnon custodi Jurisdicꝯōīs decani et capitłi Duꝝ dari. Quas injūctiones quidem et moniꝯōes sinodales decūs Re^{dus} pr̄ decrevit et mandavit observari, exequi ꝓ totum clerū̓ totius dioc. Dunelm3 ᵱdict sub penis in eisdm̄ contentis, et monuit totū̓ clerum ᵱdict acceptare copias monicoūm et injūctionum sinodáliꝝ hūmōi expensis comūnibus pochnor cujuslit ꝓoche 7 cap^{nie}. Ae etiaꝝ pnūciavit oēs 7 sīglos hm̄ōī clicos non comparentes contumaces 7 in penam contumaciar. suar. hm̄ōī eos 7 cor. quemlibet excōīcavit in scriptis put plenius patet, de ex tenore schedule ꝑ dcm̄ Re^{dum} pr̄em lect 7 subsequeñ.

In Dei nōīe amen, Nos Richus diā ꝑvidentia Duꝝ Epūs ritè ꞏ7 łetre pꝯedeꝝ oēs 7 siglos rcōres viċios 7 curatos quor. nōīa in rotulo sinodali continentur, 7 qui in dꝯō rotulo absētes annotantur, ꝓpter iꝓor. cōtumacioas in non compendo coraꝝ nob. istis die 7 loco ad subeundꝰ hanc nr̄am sacro scꝉam sinodum aꝉs in choat 7 celebraꝝ legitie᾽ monitos prius ᵱconizatos

diutiusq̄ expectatos 7 nullo modo cōpareñ p̄nūcia-
mus cōtumaces 7 coñ quēlibt cōtumacem 7 in penam
cōtumaciañ suañ h̄moi eos 7 coñ quemlibt excōica-
mus in hiis scriptis.

Tenores monicōum 7 injūctionum sinodaliñ pducñ
seqūntur in p̄xima pagina sequente.

𝖂𝖍𝖎𝖈𝖍 𝖜𝖍𝖊𝖓 𝖙𝖗𝖆𝖓𝖘𝖑𝖆𝖙𝖊𝖉 𝖗𝖚𝖓𝖓𝖊𝖙𝖍 𝖙𝖍𝖚𝖘 :

n Tuesday, viz. the first day of October in
the year of our Lord 1577 at the usual
place in the Galilee of the Cathedral
Church of Durham in presence of the the reverend
father in Christ the Lord Richard by divine providence Bishop of Durham holding his solemn Synod
with the whole clergy of his diocese of Durham aforesaid in the presence of me Christopher Chaitor notary public &c.

In which day and place the said [reverend] father
Richard after the end of the sermon in the usual
way commanded that his whole clergy aforesaid
should be summoned by the crier and when they had
been so summoned the same reverend father, after
his paternal exhortation had been made to all the
clergy then present, gave and furnished certain his
synodal monitions and injunctions written on parch-

B

ment which he handed to me Christopher Chaitor notary public aforesaid to be read of which monitions and injunctions so read the same reverend father directed copies to be given to Master Robert Swifte his vicar general in spirituals and to the Archdeacons as well of Durham as of Northumberland and also to the warden of the jurisdiction of the dean and Chapter of Durham. The which injunctions and monitions synodal the said [reverend] father Richard decreed and commanded to be observed [&] executed by the whole clergy of the whole diocese of Durham aforesaid under the penalties in the same contained and he warned the whole clergy aforesaid to receive copies of such like monitions and injunctions synodal at the common cost of the parishioners of every parish and chapelry. And also he pronounced contumacious all and singular such like clergy as made no appearance and those of this sort and such of them he denounced in the penalty of their contumacy even as appeared more fully in the record [&] from the tenor of the schedule following read by the said reverend father.

In the name of God, amen. We Richard, by divine providence bishop of Durham rightly and duly do pronounce all and singular the rectors vicars and curates whose names are contained in the roll of the synod and who are marked absent on the said roll by reason of their contumacy in not appearing before us in that place and day to undergo this our solemn synod ...... commenced and holden they having been lawfully monished, summoned afore by proclamation and for a long time waited for and in no wise appearing to be contumacious and of them each one to be contumacious and in the penalty of such their contumacy them and each of them do we denounce by this writing.

Bp Barnes's Jniunctions to the Clergy & Chu: wardens of D.D.

Certeyne moniĉ̃ons 7 injũctions geven by vs Richarde by goddes divine pvidence Busshop of Duresme to the Clergie and Churchwardens within our dioces 7 to everie of them respectivelie in our Sinode by vs celebrated 7 holden at Duresme in the gallelee within our cathedrall churche ther on Tewesdaie the first daie of October 1577. and the first yeare of our translaĉõn to the sea of Duresme afforesaid, as followethe.

First we monishe 7 straitlie enjoyne 7 com̃aund that all 7 singler the quenes majesties injũctions be in all respectes dulye 7 fully observed pformed 7 fulfilled of all 7 singler psons to whome the same doethe appertayne vnder the paynes 7 censures eccɦiasticall.

Itm̃ that the psons, vicars, curates 7 churchwardens doe within their severall pishes taike order
7 see that the blessed Sacram̃te of the body 7 blode
of our Saviŏ Jesu christe be reverentlie mīstred 7
receyved in every pishe churche at least once eṽy
monethe, 7 that they see and diligently loke that
all 7 every theire pishoners beinge above xiiij yeres of
aige do openly receyve the holly cōīon in their pishe
churche at least thrise everye yere, whereof at the
feast of Easter to be once. And if any shall not receyve the holly cōīon thrise as abovesaid, that they
faill not to maik dew p̃sentment of the names and
surnames of suche yerely at the generall Synode
holden after easter.

Itm̃ that no notorious adulterer, fornicator, in-
cestuous pson, filthie 7 com̃on drūkarde, horrible
swerers, or blasphemers of the name of god, curser
or banner, or beater of father or mother, or knowne
usurer, or any other notorious open evill liver be
admitted to the holly cōīon before they shall first
be re-converted reconciled or punished. And we
monishe 7 require eṽy pson, vicar, 7 curate within
his severall cure that wheresoever they shall note or
pceyve any to be suspected to be suche offendor,
they furthwith taikinge the churchwardens with
them goe to suche suspected pson 7 seke by all
meanes to reduce suche offendo', 7 to reclayme him,

if they can. If they can not so doe, that then they furthwith maik p̄sentm̄t therof to the ordinary or to the quenes Com̄issioners' highnes for causes eccliasti-call within the said dioces of Duresme.

Itm̄² we monishe 7 straitlie charge that none be admitted to the holly com̄unyon wᶜʰ are not confirmed 7 wᶜʰ cannot say the cathechisme p̄fitely, if that said p̄son be under thaige of xxx yeres 7 that none above xxx yeres be thervnto admitted oneles they can p̄fectly saye the Lords prayer, tharticles of the xtēn faith 7 the ten com̄aundmēts 7 that none be suffered to be maried or become a godfather or godmother to any infant at baptisme, but as afforesaid. And we streitly charge 7 com̄aunde that the p̄sons vicars 7 curates do diligently every sondaie for the space of an hower before evening prayer in the churches 7 chappels teache the children 7 yonge folkes the cathechisme, examyne 7 appose them in the same, 7 that yerely at every synode 7 gñall chapter they shall give the names of all parents, maisters & dames that shall refuse or defer to sende their children, servants, 7 apprentises to learne the cathechisme, 7 all suche as beinge sent shall stubburnelie refuse to learne or be taught the same.

Itm̄ that no cōīons or com̄emoracȏns (as some call them) be said for the dead, or at the burials of the dead, or anyversaries or monethes myndes, be

vsed for the dead, nor any supfluous ringinge at
burials, nor any supfluous ringinge on all Saints daie
at night, or on the followinge daie of old supstitiously
called all sowles daie.

𝕴tm² that no popishe abrogated hollydaies be
kept hollydaies, nor any divine servise publiquely
saide or celebrated on any suche daies, nor any supfluous faste be vsed as those called the Lady fast
saint trinyons fast, the black faste, Saint Margaret
fast or suche other invented by the devill to the dis-
honõringe of God, 7 damnacõn of the sowles of
idolotrous 7 supstitious psons.

𝕴tm² that no rites or ceremonies be vsed at the
mīstracõn of the sacramēts 7 celebracõn of divine
servise other then ar expressely set downe 7 prescribed in the booke of comon prayer, and admīstra-
cõn of sacramētes, or any ther pscribed be omitted
or neglected or left vnvsed ; 7 that the psons vicars
7 curates at ministracõn of sacramēts were cleane
7 comelie surplesses, 7 that they abrode do were
grave clerkely 7 decent apparell, as gownes or cloks
with sleves of sad coloʳ 7 none vnsemely apparell
as great ruffes, great britches, gascogne hose, scal-
ings, nor any other like monstrous 7 vnsemely apparell : comely round cloks when they ride, to cast of
the myer 7 dust may be vsed but no otherwise.
And we require 7 charge yow in the lorde that yow

by all meanes indever your sellves to frame your lives 7 coūsacōns so that ye may be lyvelie paternes, 7 holesome examples to your flockes, in all modestie, sobrietie, zeale, faithe, 7 godly conūsacōn.

Itm̃ that no medwifes nor any other women be suffred to minister babtisme ; but if the infants be waike 7 the parents likewise that they cannot exspecte the sabboth daie, that the minister, or some other godly 7 discrete pson (in that extreme necessitie onely) doe babtize suche infants at home. And that yowe herof admonishe yopr pishoñs 7 ther withall also teache them that if any infant dye without publiq̢ babtisme first to it ministred, that the same is not to be condemned or adjudged as a damned sowle: but to be well hoped of, 7 the body to be interred in the churche yearde, yet without ringinge, or any divine servyce or solemnity bycause the same was not solemnely p̃fessed 7 receyved into the church 7 congregacōn. And we charge 7 comaunde yow duly frome tyme to tyme to p̃sent the names 7 surnames of all suche women as shall taike in hande or enterp̃ce to babtize, or at the childes birthes vse supsticious ceremonyes, orizons, charmes, or develishe rytes, or sorceries.

Itm̃ that no psons, vicars, curates, or other psons eccliasticall beinge vnmaried doe hereafter reteyne or kepe any women in his or their howses or

howse other then suche as ar allowed by the injūctions nor that any of them do hante or frequente any
comōon tavernes or aile howses, or any vnlawfull
games, as cardinge, dicinge, bowlinge, dauncinge or
suche like, or any fence scholes, may games, nor that
any of their mansion howses be kept as Aile-howses,
tavernes, or howses of gamynge, 7 suche evill rule.
And that their howses 7 chancels be furthwith repared, 7 that they setle themselves to thuttermost
of their habilytie to kepe goddly hospitalities, 7 doe
not let out, lease out, or taverne out their livings
vnder payne of depꝓvation 7 other censures eccliasti-
ticall.

Ꜹtmꝰ that all 7 everye the psons 7 vicars within this our said dioces of Duresme doe diligently
attende 7 taike care that their cures and churches
be well 7 duly served 7 with none other but with
suche as first shall bringe, 7 openly shewe to them or
to the churchewardens our licence vnder the subscription of our name, or vnder our seall for causes eccli-
ásticall within this our said dioces comōonly vsed, nor
shall suffer or pmitt any to teache scholes either
publiqꝛly or ꝓvately, in any ꝓvate howses within their
pishes onles they shall bringe licenses first frome vs
vnder our hande 7 afforesaid seall: But if any shall
otherwise attempte, shall boaithe inhibite them 7
furthwith ꝓsent their names 7 surnames 7 the howse

where they shall be receyved vnto us or our vicar g̃nall : And likewise that no forreyne preacher, that is to say, straunge preacher, 7 not resiant within our dioces shal be receyved or admitted to preache in any of your p̃she churches, chappels, or other places, onles they shall bringe first our testimoniall frome vs of their subscription to the orders 7 articles by her highnes speciall direction to vs p̃scribed in this behalf.

Itm̃² that all 7 every psons, vicars, 7 curates within or of this our said dioces which shall not be licensed as is afforesaide to preache shall duly payne-fully 7 frely teache the children of their severall p̃shes 7 cures to reade and write. And suche as they shall by good 7 due tryall finde to be apte to learne 7 of pregnant capacitie, then they shall exhorte their parentes to set them to scholes and learnynge of the good 7 liberall sciences. And suche as they shall trye to be vnapte 7 no pregnant witt nor good capa-citie, they shall move 7 require their parents to sett to learne husbandry or other good craftes that yet so they may growe to be good mēbers to the country 7 com̃on weall. And we will 7 com̃aunde that the said psons vicars 7 curates, 7 eṽy of them shall at least every yeare once in Lent, or els so often as they shall thinke good expedient 7 true, examyne all 7 every their p̃shoners whome they shall thinke

mete of their skille 7 knowlede of their dewtie to god
7 their neighbour, of the articles of their faithe, 7
the x cõmaundemēts of god 7 their vnderstandinge
of the cathechismo 7 affection in religion. And
whomesoever they shall fynde defective in that behalf they shall vnto such either give short 7 expedient tyme to learne or seclude them from receyvinge
of the holly cōĩon aftʳ they shall refuse to learne or
be instructed, 7 of their doings in this behalf they
shall duely certify 7 advertize vs at eͧy s. sinode, or
s. chapterȠ.

Ꝉtm̃ we ordayne constitute 7 decree that yerelie
their shal be two generall synodes celebrated 7 hold-
en at Duresme in the Galele thence tȟ one on the
tuesdaie next followinge the first sondaie after easter,
7 the other on the first tuesdaie after the feast of St.
Michaell tharchangell yerely. At wᶜʰ we streitly
enjoyne 7 charge all 7 singlar psons vicars 7 curats
ministers 7 deacons to be psonally p̃sent 7 attendant
then 7 their to doe 7 receyve as the nature of the
Synodes require. And likewise that yerelie our
chauncelor or vicar generall shall at some convenient
churche within eͧy warde 7 deanery within this our
said dioces celebrate 7 kepe two generall chapters:
the one alwaies to be holden, 7 kept within the
monethe of Ianuarye, 7 the other in the monethe
of Iulye, wherat (beinge assisted by our Archdeacons

within their severall offices, 7 by our referendarye
by vs to be named 7 assigned) examynačõn shall be
had of the progresse in learnynge 7 studyenge of the
scriptures of the psons, vicars, 7 curats, ministers 7
deacons 7 exercises 7 tasks shall be enjoyned to
them, 7 required of them 7 inquisičõn shal be maide
of their maners, lives, conversačõns, 7 demeano" 7 of
the due execučõn of their offices 7 servinge of their
cures. And at the same the churche wardens shal
be called to p̃sent all faltes 7 defaltes done or ppe-
trated contrary to theis our monič õns or any pte of
the same : And all such compertes to be exhibited
7 presented to us w^{th}in viij daies after thende of the
said monethes of Ianuarye 7 Iuly, 7 either of them.

Itm̃ we monishe 7 streitlye enjoyne that at the
begyñynge of every suche chapter ther shal be a
sermon, 7 after the same shal be songe the hymne
intituled, Come holy ghost eternall god p̃cedinge
&c And after the same especiall prayers to be
maide for the quenes majestie, for the churche, the
prosperous estaite of the comõn weall 7 good suc-
cesse 7 increase of religion 7 of the gospell &c And
for the afflicted 7 p̃secuted mēbers of the churche.
And that done then p̃ceade to the chapter to celebrate the same, first openly readinge the quenes
ma^{ties} Injūctions 7 theise our monič õns 7 exactinge

p̃sentmēts of the churchwardens thereupon, 7 then
to thexamynaċõn of the clergie.

Ἴtm᷉ we monishe 7 straitly charge 7 comãunde all
7 singłer psons vicars 7 curates within our dioces
that at the leaste iiij tymes yerelie the openly upon
some sondaies in tyme of divine service give warn-
inge vnto their pishoſs that yonge folkes by the
lawes of god may not mary without consent of their
parents 7 that no yonge man haithe power to con-
tracte matrimony before he be fully xvi yeres of aige,
nor any woman before she be fully xiiij yeres of aige,
7 that all p̃vie contracts ar against the lawes, 7 the
offenders ar sharpelie 7 severely to be punyshed.

Ἴtm᷉ that yow the psons vicars 7 curates doe dulie
7 dilegently note 7 p̃sente vnto vs in. writinge at
every Sinode 7 generall chapter the names 7 surnames of all such psons eccliasticall preistes or deacons, as have relinquished 7 left of the ministery, or
refuse to minister, giving themselves to seculer func-
tions, as to be gardiners, stewards to gentlemen, or
suche like, or as walke in laymens apparell, disguysed.
And also who receyvethe relevethe, harborethe, or
reteyneth any suche disloyall psons 7 of their con-
venticles.

Ἴtm᷉ we monishe yow that yow doe not solemnize
mr̃õny betwene any psons frome the first sondaie in

Lent vntill the first sondaie after Easter, nor betwene any psons vnles the bannes shal be first
solemnely published thre severall sondaies or hollydaies, 7 therupon no lawfull impedimēt founde, nor
betwene any notorious advlterer or fornicator before
they shal be reconciled, nor betwene any psons within
the degrees of consanguinitie and affynyty by the
lawes p̄hibited.

 Itm̄ we streitlie charge 7 comāunde that none of
our Archedeacons chauncelors or comissaries or any
other psons occupieing or exercisinge eccliasticall
jurisdiction within our dioces of Duresme in any
places exempte or not exempte shall comūte any
penaunce or correction for syn, or any eccliasticall
cryme or offence into any pecuniary some or taike
any money or somes of money for releasinge the
same under the paynes of dep̄vacon frome their livings, 7 jurisdictions, or other censures eccliasticall
by vs to be inflicted.

Mon.

Monicons especially given to the churchewardons of eu'y p'ishe within this our said dioces of Duresme w'ch we streitly charge all & single the p'sons vicars & curates of this our said dioces quarterly duly to publishe to the churchewardons & p'ishoners within their severall Cures, and to attende that they execute the same.

Imprimis we monishe 7 enjoyne that the churchewardōs shall be yerely upon the assention daie chosen 7 vpon the sonday then next ensueinge shal be openlie sworne by the pson, vicar, or curate in the presence of the pishoffs that daie 7 tyme in the churche assombled at prayer 7 divine service wᶜʰ sondaie affore eveninge prayers we do assigne for the churche wardons of the former yere to give vp 7 maik a full 7 pfecte accompte of their receptes 7 expenses abowte the churches affaires the last yere by them laid out : 7 shall maike full paymēt to the handes of the new sworne churchewardens of all somes of money remayninge in their hands or charge, 7 full delyvery of all churche goodds books 7 other implemētes 7 furnitures, wᶜʰ do apperteyne to their churche vnto the said new churchwardons, which accompte paymēt 7 delyvery we comaund to be registred in the register booke. And we will 7 comaunde that the othe written after theise our injūctions be duly ministred to the churchewardens, as is afforesaid.

Itm̃ we monishe charge 7 comaunde the churchewardens of eᵛy pishe 7 chappell that they diligently

7 faithfully attend to the due execuçõn of all 7 every the Quenes majesties Injūctyons 7 theise our moni-çõns, 7 faithefully at eûy generall chapter p̄sent the names 7 surnames of all 7 singuler the violaters 7 transgressors of the same without pcialitie of what estate degre or callinge soever the same shal be.

℣tm̄ we monishe 7 charge that they taike dili-gent care 7 present order that their churches 7 chappels be well repared 7 clenly kept, that they have all necessaries 7 comely furnitures 7 imple-mētes, 7 all books requisite before xrēnmas next vn-der paynes of interdiction 7 suspençõn to be p̄noun-ced against themselves ; And that all balkes or herses whervpon lightes or serges were in tyme of poperye vsed to be sett, 7 all the remanents of Roode lofts, 7 remanents of alters, 7 all corbell stones whervpon images have been placed be vtterly removed out of the churches 7 chappels before xrēn-mas next, 7 the places where they stode, p̄getted over with lyme vnder the paynes afforesaid.

℣tm̄ that the churchwardens taike order, 7 dili-gently see that no faires, or marketts be holden or kept vpon sondaies : nor any pedler or other open, or sell any waires in any churches, churche porches, or churche yeardes at any tyme at all, nor in any place in tyme of divine service of sermons or minis-traçõn of sacramēts, nor that duringe suche tymes any begger be suffered to sitt, lye, or stande begging abrode : nor that any tavernes, aile howses or victualinge howses duringe such tyme be kept open, or any victuall solde, nor any gamynge vsed, but if any psons whatsoever shall offende against any parte of this our moniõõn they wilh convenient spedo 7 duly p̃sent the same.

The furnitures, implemẽts 7 bookes requisite to be had in every churche 7 so cõmaunded by publiq, authoritie.

Jmplemẽtes.

A decent cõĩon table upon a frame.

A decent Baptisterie or fonte.

A decent pulpit.

A convenient place for the minister to say divine service at.

A chist with thre lockes for the poore.

Furnituꝛes.

Cleane lynnynge clothes for the comunion table.

A coveringe for the same of Buckerhm̃ or suche lyke.

A comely surplesse.

A cõĩon cuppe of silver with a cover.

Bookes.

A Bible of the largest volume, a comunion booke likewise.

Two psalter Bookes, the two books of Homylies.

The postils, The quenes majesties Injunctions, the tables of degrees of consanguinitie 7 affinytie allowed 7 forbidden for mariage.

A Register Booke, the defence of the appology.

And thes our monicons.

The othe wch the psons vicars & curates shall minister to the churche wardons.

Now that be chosen to be churchewardens of this churche or chappell for this next yere doe swere by god 7 the holly gospel before yow laide, that yow shall execute the said office effectuallie 7 diligently to the advancemēte of goddes glorie 7 the comoditie of this churche 7 pishe. The Quenes Injūctions 7 the ordinaries monicons ye shall observe, 7 so far as in yow liethe cause others to observe, And the violators of the same, yow shall duelye 7 without all ptialitie psent 7 detecte to the Quenes highnes cōmissions for causes eccliasticall within this dioces, or to the jurates 7 sworne men, or to the chauncelo[r]. And yow shall yeilde 7 give up at the yeres ende a faithefull 7 true accompte of all somes by yowe re-

ceyved 7 laide out for the use of this churche, 7 all
suche somes of money, churche implemētes, furnitures, 7 bookes, as then shall remayne vnder your
charge, yow shall faithfully 7 fully paie over 7 delyver to yoͬ souccesso's; so god yow helpe by Jesu
christ.

That done the minister shall openlie reade vnto
them the quenes Injūctions 7 the ordinaries moniĉōns.

All 7 singler the wᶜ our moniĉōns afforesaid given
to our said Clergie be in nūber xvij. And all 7
singler our afforesaid moniĉōns given to the churchewardens in nūber iiij We the said Reverende father
repeatinge the same in forme nature 7 strenghe of
moniĉōns and injūctions doe publishe 7 give streitly
charginge the same 7 eͮy clause pte 7 pcell of the
same of all 7 eͮy our afforesaid Clergie, churchewardons 7 others respectivelie to be duely inviolablely
7 fully observed fulfilled 7 kept, under the paynes of
excōĩcaĉōn, suspenĉōn, interdiction 7 other censures
ecctiasticall. In witnes wherof unto thes ꝑsents we
have sett to our greater seall. Geven at Duresme
in the gallele in Sinode their celebrated on the
tewesdaie the first daie of October as before is noted.
decreinge copies 7 true transcripts hereof to be frely
delyvered to our vicar gñall 7 to our Archedeacons
of Duresme and Northumberland, to the keper of
the peculier ecctiasticall jurisdiction of the deane of
Duresme, 7 the chapter. And then with all conve-

nient spede to delyver copies herof to eỼy pishe 7 chappelrie within our said dioces, receyving onely viij^d for eủy copye to be paid by the Curate 7 churchewardens by equall porc̃õns for the writinge therof, 7 no more.

Colla̎c̃õne diligenti facta concordant hæ suprascriptæ monic̃õnes cum monic̃õnibus originalibus in archivis epãlibus Dunelm̃ remanentibus.

Eꝗpme Giłbtum Spence notariũ publicum.

The wayfarings of Ralph Thoresby in the North of England.

IMPRINTED BY M. A. RICHARDSON,
IN GREY STREET, NEWCASTLE.
MDCCCXLVIII.

ONLY 100 COPIES PRINTED.

TO

THE REV. JOSEPH HUNTER, F.S.A., &c.,

THIS ANNOTATED REPRINT OF A PORTION OF THE

DIARY AND CORRESPONDENCE OF THE

HISTORIAN OF LEEDS, WHICH AS A WHOLE

RECEIVED THE ADVANTAGE OF HIS

EDITORIAL SUPERINTENDENCE,

IS RESPECTFULLY DEDICATED

BY THE EDITOR.

HE following tract is founded upon the Diary and Correspondence of Ralph Thoresby the Historian of Leeds, so excellently edited by the Rev. Joseph Hunter. Our object in the present reprint is further to annotate that portion which relates to the northern counties of England, and so impart that additional value to the text which local knowledge is alone able to confer.

G. B. R. at Newcastle, this February, mdccclxxiii.

During the seventeenth century it was a prevailing fashion for persons possessed of any amount of literary or contemplative disposition, to keep diurnal records of their own acts and feelings, and the current events of their time, and we owe a debt of gratitude to such persons for placing in our hands a mass of information locally valuable, antecedent to the days in which our newspapers first took cognizance of domestic occurences. Among the most distinguished of these useful personages was Ralph Thoresby the Historian of Leeds, who in his mercantile transactions as a woollen draper, made frequent journeys into Durham, Northumberland, and Newcastle-upon-Tyne, and indeed these places had closer ties upon him than those of mere profit, for though the principal branch of his fa-

mily were and had long been seated in his native
county of York, yet he had connections at Brafferton
in Durham, a cousin and many intimate friends in
Newcastle upon Tyne, and property at Rock in
Northumberland. His visits to these places were,
therefore, as might be expected, very numerous, des-
pite the tedious mode of transit then in use. As it
is no part of our present business to trace the history of our writer, we will at once commence with
his first *recorded* visit to our district in the twenty-
first year of his age. On this occasion, he with his
father set off from Leeds, 17 April, 1679, "towards
Newcastle, and so to Rock and Berwick, experienc-
ing all along the goodness of God in our preservation." Such phraseology, suitable perhaps at any
time, was particularly so at this, when we consider
the state of the roads, if such they could be called,
and the slow and precarious mode of travelling,
both affording every incouragement to the infliction
of highway robbery, and even of murder. In a similar strain, therefore, he exclaims on the ninth day
after, "we returned safe home, Laus Deo!"

Six months after this, the sudden death of his
father devolved the concerns and cares of the whole
family upon him. He undertook to proceed with
the business left by his parent, in whose house he
continued to reside, and had a younger brother and

sister in household with him. Probably in order to arrange his affairs consequent upon the decease of his parent, he occurs 5 April, 1680, "making ready writings, &c., for the north," and after dinner setting forth with his uncle Michael Idle, reaching Borough-bridge in the evening. On the ensuing day he pass-ed through Northallerton, and so into Darlington, where he expected to have met Captain Widdring-ton.* On the seventh, he describes getting to Dur-ham early, and having despatched his business with the captain, and visited his relatives there, got well to Newcastle. "Newcastle," says he, "was the place formerly much delighted in, and earnestly de-sired, for my dear relations there; but now, it is an

* Captain Edward Widdrington of Felton, co. Northd., as the text itself afterwards informs us. 16 June, 1680, Thoresby occurs being with him in London "about the business which chiefly occa-sioned the journey" thither. 21 to 26. Every day employed either about my concerns at Rock with Captain Widdrington, &c.," and under the 27th of the same month, he has "most of this week spent in business with Captain Widdrington, Sir Richard Stott, &c. the rest in visits, buying things, transcribing monuments in West-minster Abbey, in which I can better excuse myself than in staying so late on Saturday night at Captain Widdrington's, where was too great plenty of the strongest liquors, which affected me by their con-quest of my friend, which being partly on my account, I desire may be for my humiliation." On 17 July, he tells us (having then re-turned to Leeds), "writing, and taken up with stating Rock ac-counts. Lord, help me to be the better for the greater plenty and prosperity that I enjoy; and not like the worldling, either to set my heart thereon, to be more negligent in spiritual things." On 19 July, he mentions consulting "with J. Robinson, about Northern tenants, and writing to Captain Widdrington," &c.—(*Thoresb. Diar.*)

B

aggravation to my sorrow, to remember past com-
forts and present slights." He left this place however, on the next day, and reached home on the
ninth, when he states "I found my poor desolate
family all well; but, alas! the fresh remembrance
of our unutterable loss is most bitter, and almost
insupportable."

On 5 May, 1680, he occurs consulting Lawyer
Rookby (afterwards Sir Thomas Rokeby, and a
Judge) about his Northumberland affairs, which
would appear to have given him much trouble at this
time,[b] and on the 17th in company with Michael
Idle, "carried pretty sister Abigail (her dear father's
picture) along with me, and got safe to Darlington,
forty long miles, and yet she not at all weary."
On the 19th they left Newcastle for Morpeth, and
thence to Alnwick, where they lodged for the night,
and on the next day rode to his estate at Rock,
where they dispatched their business, though in
haste, and returned to Alnwick the same day. On
the ensuing day (21) they arrived at Newcastle

[b] On 5 Ap. 1682, Thoresby mentions that he spent the "forenoon with Cousin Thoresby's, of Sykehouse, who, notwithstanding
former unkindnesses, (endeavours to deprive me of the estate in the
north) have been very welcome in their present straits to my house,
but have exceedingly straitened me for time about better things,
and made me lose much of that precious commodity in every respect."—(Thoresb. Diar.)

where says he, "having stayed three or four hours, we rid to Durham; there I got a sight again of my poor sister. Natural affections wrought sore, and she could not forbear weeping at our parting, which made my very heart bleed within me, and my too violent affections were so strong, that I slept not an hour all night, the inconveniences whereof I found the next day." On the 23d. they left for home in a storm of wind and rain.

He again occurs visiting the north in Sept. 1680: on the 13th of that month he tells us that he "set forward, though melancholy, and all alone, towards Durham, baited at Northallerton, and got well to Darlington.—14. Got to Durham pretty early; and found my poor sister, and all relations pretty well. 15. Enjoyed the converse of friends; then dined at Cousin Walker's,ᶜ went afterwards to see the Abbey.; viewed the exceedingly rich copes and robes, was troubled to see so much superstition remaining in Protestant Churches; tapers, basins, and richly embroidered I. H. S. upon the high altar, with the picture of God the Father, like an old man; the

---

ᶜ Elsewhere, "Cousin Michael Walker." In these days the phrase *cousin* had so wide a signification that it is difficult to determine what amount of relationship is here meant. We find, however, that Tabitha Thursby, widow of Michael Walker, became in 1690, the second wife of Henry Eden of Shincliffe, M.D. She was buried 1699.—(*Sharp MS.*)

Son, as a young man, richly embroidered upon their copes. Lord, open their eyes, that the substance of religion be not at length turned into shadows and ceremonies! 16. Advising with Aunt &c., returned from Durham to Allerton," and thence home the next day.

On 28 December, 1680, he occurs being at Bishop-Auckland where he says he "transcribed the epitaph of Bishop Cousins,[d] interred in a stately chapel of his own foundation; thence to Durham, without prejudice, though the ways very deep and the night dark. 29. Dined at cousin Walker's, and stayed most of the day there, with relations. 31. Rid with Cousin to Newcastle. 1 Jan. Afternoon returned to Durham. 2 Die Dom. In the forenoon went to the minster; was somewhat amazed at their ornaments, tapers, rich embroidered copes, vestments, &c. Dr. Brevin, a native of France,[e] discoursed of the birth of Christ; went after to Shinkley, and heard a discourse from Mr. Dixon, Colos. iij. 3. 3. Rid

[d] Thoresby on another occasion describes himself "epitomizing Bishop Cousins's life and drawing his picture;" and says "he was a noble benefactor, and I hope a more sincere Protestant than some would insinuate."—(Thoresb. Diar.)

[e] Daniel Brevint, A.M. succeeded in 1660 as prebendary of the tenth stall on the promotion of Cosin to the see. He was presented by Charles II. He was also rector of Branspeth, and died dean of Lincoln, 5 May, 1695.—(Surtees Dur., Sharp MS.)

with relations to cousin Paxton's, at Shinkley; dined there, and returned safe to Durham. 5. Set forwards pretty early; found the ways worst at first, but afterwards tolerable, so got well home."

In July, 1681, he occurs visiting Harrogate for the benefit of his health, and tell us that the company there on the 8th and 9th of the month "was better furnished than ordinary, with Sir Ralph Jennyson of Newcastle, and his lady,*(my dear father and uncle's friends,) and others."

In September, 1681, he visited the north in company with Mr. Hickson; on the 6th he says "we rode to Burrowbridge, and thence to Topcliffe, when supposing we should not stay long, left my charged pistols in the bags, which at my mounting again, being gone, caused a great jealousy of some des'gn against us; and the rather, because Mr. H. and his debtor had come to high words, and the landlord took the debtor's part, and denied to send for the ostler, till upon some brisk compliments, we were just for riding to depose upon oath before Sir M. Robinson, and then in the very same straw we had sought carefully before, they were found, and one of

---

* Sir Ralph Jennison of Elswick, knight, and a Justice of Peace for the county of Northumberland. Lady Jane Jenison was buried in the church of S. Nicholas, 30 March, 1699, and sir Ralph (in the same church) on 11 Ap. 1701.—*(Sessions pprs. Nd., Reg. S. Nich.)*

them where the horse could not get to ; which more
fully manifested the knavery, as also their leaving,
for a pretence, the red bags in the holster ; but we
got very well, though late, to Northallerton that
night.   7. Thence by Darlington to Durham ;
whence, after a short stay with relations in Newcastle, but did little business.   8. Morning, visited
some drapers in order to their accounts ; then went
with E[leazar] H[odshon]ᶠ down to Shields by water,

ᶠ This we have presumed to be intended for Eleazar Hodshon,
whose name is given in full a few paragraphs further on, as
accompanying Thoresby northward from Edinburgh.   Eleazar
was the son of Mathew, who may have been that Mathew (son of
George, merchant) who was baptized on 25 Jan. 1628-9 at the
church of All Saints.   Eleazar was apprenticed 2 Feb. 1664-5 to Gil-
bert Browell, barber-chirurgeon, but on 17 June, 1668, made choice
of Peter Baites, and having fully served his time, was admitted to
the freedom of the company, 3 May, 1672.   In this or the following
year he married his first wife Alice, by whom he had Matthew, bap.
27 Aug. 1674, and Elizabeth, bap. 15 July 1676, in giving birth to
whom it is probable his wife laid down her own life, for she was
buried 22 July following.   His second wife Dorothy, he certainly
married previous to 1692, on 29 March in which year he himself
was buried.   It is probable his widow was not left in the best of
circumstances as 9 June, 1718, she occurs receiving at the hands of
the company, the sum of five shillings, in consequence, we may
fairly presume, of her necessitous condition : she was buried 21
Sep. 1721.   If we do not mistake our evidence, Hodshon acted as
sheriff's sergeant, in which capacity it is not improbable we find him
in his connection with Thoresby.   On 18 March, 1678-9, the company
of Butchers retain him as inspector of flesh-meat in the public market in order to the burning of such as should be found unwholesome;
but on Ash Wednesday, 1691, they discharge him from the office.
In 1680 he occurs in his capacity of serjeant under Joseph Bonner,
sheriff, signing an acquittance to the company of Weavers, one of
whose members had been imprisoned in the jail of New-Gate ; and

but it proved a most terrible stormy day—visited
Tinmouth Castle, now almost ruined, and maintained
by a slender garrison; and the new fort called Clif-

11 March, 1683-4, was appointed by the Hostmen, one of the seizors
of coals shipped by unfree coal owners or fitters—a post to which
his experience as a public officer would seem to have entitled him,
as he was not a member of that fraternity. Of what might have
been supposed his more congenial profession of a chirurgeon, we
have but few memorials, and these relate rather to his disputes with
the fellowship or infractions of their rules (cognizance not being
taken of anything else) than to his talents in the healing art.
Whatever notions we may form of the surgeon of our own days,
what are we to think of the barber-chirurgeon of antiquity who in
sending in his yearly bill to his patient would set out with charges
for administering potions, pills, tinctures, and plasters to the
diseased frame; next would follow the costs of repeated bleeding,
or daily or weekly shaving; then those of polling, and perchance
those of washing and scrubbing; and winding up with an item for
so many pounds of tallow candles! In 1675 we find that one
Jacob Grieve, a foreign chirurgeon, who was an apprentice to Thomas
Skinner of the city of Durham, and whose time was not fully served,
had "lately come to this towne of Newcastle, and married here, and
hath a family, and hath made some private contract and secret
agreement with Eleazar Hodshon barber chirurgeon, and under that
colour manadge the whole afaire, and now the said Eleazar Hodshon pretends Jacob Grieve is his apprentice bound by indentures,
all which dealings are nothing but deceipt and fraud. 1st. That
the said Jacob Grieve is bound by indentures by Skinner as abovesaid. 2. He is likewise bound by indentures as an apprentice to
one in London. 3. He is married, maintains his wife and family,
and lives of himself. 4. Jacob Grieve is already master of the
trade and needs no learning or instruction from Eleazar Hodshon.
5. Eleazar Hodshon neither ownes, workes nor labours in the shopp,
but in all probabilitie for a little money paid or secured him doth
shelter, cloake, and colour the illegal actings and contrivances aforesaid." In consequence of this, the company ordered 29 Aug. 1679,
that Hodshon or any other brother should be debarred from em-
ploying Grieve on pain of 40s. a month, and that proceedings be
instituted against him should he any longer practise within the

fords', fortified with thirty culverins, and ten demi-
culverins, under the government of the earl of Newcastle ; in the evening not daring, without imminent
hazard, as the ship-master said, to return by water,
were forced to hire horses and return by land to
Newcastle !   9. Morning, finishing my business
with some drapers; went to Sandgate to enquire of,
and receive some out-rents, and at return, took horse
for Northumberland; about five miles off, transcribed
some verses from a monumental pillar, erected in
the highway, by John Pigg,[a] the mathematician;

town.   In 1686, Hodshon again occurs offending the fraternity in a
similar manner by harbouring a young man named Robert Hads-
worth whom he pretended was a freeman of York : this he was
ordered to prove or pay the usual monthly fine of 40s. as before.

We may as well mention that Henry, son of an Eleazar Hodshon,
who is described as late of Stella, co. Dur. gentleman deceased, was
apprenticed to William Hutchinson, of Newcastle, merchant adventurer and mercer.   From the similarity of name between these
persons, it is probable that they were relatives.—(*Reg. S. Nich. and
All Sts., Bbr. Chgns., Merchts., Butchers, and Hostmen's bks., Weavers'
pprs.*)

[a] John Pigg town-surveyor for Newcastle, was probably the son of
John Pigg of Newcastle, weaver, and Isabel his wife, who is mentioned as a widow Ap. 1647, when she and her son John Pigg,
weaver, join in conveying a piece of land without Pilgrim-street
gate, whereon now stands the south side of Saville Row, to William
Gibson, of the same town, merchant.   In 1647, John Pigg occurs
as surveyor, and is ordered by the council, together with John Taylor, to superintend the reparation of a water course from the Black
Friary and adjoining grounds.   Barnes tells us that he was *land*-
surveyor for the town, and as one Henry Moore occurs occupying
the same or a similar office at or during the very period in which
Pigg is understood to have held it, he probably was a species of

thence by Captain Edward Widdrington's, at Felton, to Morpeth, and after a short stay there, over
the moors to Alnwick, an ancient town fortified with
a curious castle, and an old wall. 10. By Rock;

superior officer or engineer at the period indicated, though he afterwards occurs exercising the ordinary powers of our modern officer
of the name. Thoresby, it will be seen, denominates him a mathematician, and it is very probable that his talents in this way, formed and perfected at the loom, may have recommended him to the
governing body as a person capable of effectually serving their purposes. Thoresby's language and the evident interest he takes in
our surveyor, seems to imply the possession of considerable talent,
and his hand-writing so good at a period when but few could write
at all, certainly favours this opinion. By will, dated 27 Oct. 1688,
he bequeathed three dwelling houses and their appurtenances, situate in Pilgrim-street, opposite the end of Market-street, with his
estates in Northumberland and Durham, to Robert Bewick of Close
House, co. Northd. esq.. William Hutchinson, Phineas Allen, and
Matthias Partis of Newcastle, merchants, Lancelot Cramlington of
Newcastle, gentleman, Matthew Ladler of Clifton Loaning, co.
Northd. gentleman, and John Routchester of Gateshead, boatbuilder,
in trust, for charitable purposes. In his will he states, that the poor
people on whom this charity is bestowed shall be only those who
"fear God and are of the Protestant religion, and have not cast
themselves into poverty by their idleness nor reduced themselves
to beggarye by their own riotous prodigalitye, but are by age sickness or decripednesse disabled from work; or where men have
children too numerous for their worke too maintain; for I have always observed if men will be not idle, they need not want." These excellent intentions, however, were never brought into execution:
Cramlington, the surviving trustee availed himself of his survivor-
ship and his relations came to enjoy the property. The matter was
brought into Chancery, and suitable dispositions were made, but in
after years the uses were vested in the governors of the Infirmary,
perhaps the very best way in which the bequest could have been
appropriated. By the same will he devised £5 a year to the minister of Earsdon to preach at least five times a year, £5 per annum
for the repair of such highways of Northumberland as most required
it, and to his niece Ann Rea, "for her great care and tenderness

where I found the old tenants repenting their unkind dealings and continual murmurings for abatements, which hastened the sale of the estate ; and now they would gladly have the same lands at an ordinary ad-

towards him" such sum or sums of money as his trustees should think proper. Three months after the signing of his will, he was buried at S. Andrew's, with this memorial "John Pige, January 27, 1688-9."

We are told by the editor of the MS. life of Alderman Barnes that he was "well known both to the king [Charles II.] and the duke of York, and for his giddy singularities noted not only through the country but almost thro' the kingdom. He usually wore a high-crowned hat, a strait coat, and would never ride, but walkt the pace of any horse hundreds of miles on foot with a quarter staff fenced with an iron fork at one end. Mr. Barnes was neither able to please this man, nor yet be quiet with his intoxicated whimsies. The king and duke of York, to whom he was often trotting, made themselves sport with him, as looking upon him to be a brainsick enthusiast, and he was no less. He was of so peculiar and odd a humour, that he would not only go to prison when he needed not, but conceitedly chused the vilest part of the prison for his apartment, where he continued a long while when he might have had his liberty whenever he pleased. But Heaven's Favourite as this visionary fancy'd himself, every body knew him to be cursedly covetous, and the end he made answered the disgrace he had thrown upon sufferings for religion, this Pig dying in his stye, in circumstances not unlike those who lay hands on themselves or die crazy and distracted." Another authority tells us that " at the end of the Barras Bridge before the chapel [of S. James] stood a stately cross firm and compleat, and John Pig in the time of the Rebellion took it down, and called it idolatry, and thought to make his own use of it ; but it was broke by some who hated it should be prophaned." Bourne follows in a similar strain when he says that our surveyor " built a curious stone pillar, inscribed with texts of scripture, still standing at the Three-Mile-Bridge, by the side of the Morpeth road, as a monument of his whimsical head, and which very deservedly to this day bears the name of PIGG's FOLLY !"—and Hornby, (to wind up this tirade of abuse) remarks that he was a

vancement; discoursed Mr. Clavering about the ar-
rears; thence over the moors to Belford, thence over
the Sands, where we had a fair prospect of Holy Island, to Berwick, where we got well, and in time to

noted enthusiast and that his name and peculiarities were the
theme of conversation so late as the middle of the last century.
He tells us that he has heard similar stories of him, as to his walking and imprisonment by ancient persons who lived near his time,
and had them from such as knew him personally. He also remarks upon his bequest for the repair of the roads (though he
erroneously states them to have been those between Newcastle and
London) as indicative of his passion for pedestrian exercise, and his
knowledge of the value and necessity of keeping in a proper condition those important means of communication between place and
place. "This account of honest Pigg," observes Mackenzie, alluding to the eccentricities attributed to him by Barnes, "is evidently
exaggerated: being a Puritan was sufficient to entitle him to the
scoffs of the profane, and the hatred of bigots of a different
class. The above extract from his will shews that he was not de-
ficient in discernment and good sense; and his choice of executors
implies that his connexions were respectable. He was evidently
an eccentric man; but his charitable bequests ought to have procured more indulgence for his memory." The pillar which Thoresby
and our note mentions, was situate on the north side of the Three
Mile Bridge on the great north road. It was a square structure of
stone 12½ feet high, bearing three sun dials, and covered with scraps
of holy writ and the following inscription, which we procure from
another part of Thoresby's work :—

> Who would not love thee, while they may
> Enjoy thee walking? for thy way
> Is pleasure and delight : let such
> As see thee, choose thee, prize thee much.

Pigg was in the habit of walking every morning from his house to
this place and back, and is said to have raised this column as a
token of gratitude for the health and pleasure which he received in
his daily promenade, and to have inscribed it with moral lessons
for the benefit of all who travel on this road. Mackenzie imagines
that it was the same cross which Pigg took down at the Barras-
Bridge, but the pillar in question, which probably our historian

view the town, which is ancient and ill-built, but
stands very commodiously and is well fortified. 11. Die
Dom. Being at church too early, was transcribing
some monuments, which was the first place I observed the Scotch mode for Aldermen and persons of
some rank to be buried in the church yard. The
church was built, 1652, Colonel Fenwick, their Governor, being a chief instrument (in memory of
whom there is an inscription in the church, of which,
see p. 125, of my Collections,) by procuring monies
owing to the town for soldiers pay; it has no steeple,
the old one in the midst of the town serving: the
Minister was on the different sorts of sorrow, the
benefits of the godly, and the disadvantage of the
carnal; was to visit Mr. Windlows, and after walked
around the walls. 12. Morning, from Berwick over
the Moors, where we found the proverb verified, that
a Scotch mist, for I cannot say it rained, wets the
Englishman to the skin." On the 21st of the same
month, Thoresby re-entered England by way of Carlisle : on the following day he says " viewing the cas-

---

never particularly observed, could never have formed any part of a
medieval structure, and had evidently been edified from new materials and in the architectural taste which characterized the period in
which its builder lived. Some twenty years ago a house in the
neighbourhood requiring additions or repairs, the pillar was sacri-
legiously demolished, and the stones applied to that use.—(*Bourne,
Hornby, Mackenzie, Milb. MS., Charlton Deeds, Barnes MS., Reg. S.
Andw., Corpn. bks., Infirmary repts., &c.*)

tle, an ancient structure, a seat of the present Earl
of Carlisle's; then the church, but frustrated of
my expectations, most of the monuments of antiquity
being defaced, and nothing new worth observing.
After, at a feast at Mr. Basil Fielding's;[i] then with
the mayor and several aldermen[j] of Carlisle, but
stayed too long, and drunk too freely. We made it
pretty late ere we got to Penrith, where (as at Stir-
ling) constrained to transcribe some monuments in the
church by candlelight. 23. From Penrith, leaving
Brougham Castle on the one hand, and Lowther and
Strickland, which give their names to two ancient
families, on the other, we came by a monumental
pillar, erected by Ann, Countess of Pembroke, where

[i] Can this be the Bazil Fielding (son of Israel Fielding, late of
Stratforth, in the county of York, esquire, who was apprenticed to
Myles Man of Newcastle-upon-Tyne, merchant adventurer and mercer, 10 Oct. 1647, who on 19 Feb. 1648, was set over to William
Brathwaite to serve the remainder of his time, and on 31 Dec. 1650 to
Metcalfe Rippon, but departed his masters service? Israel, another
and perhaps elder son, was apprenticed to Edward Hall of Newcastle, merchant adventurer and draper, on 15 Sep. 1647. The Ducatus Leodiensis tells us that Israel Fielding of Stratforth, esquire,
(probably the father of our Basil and Israel) married Anne, daughter of Francis Wolrich of Alconbury, esquire, (son and heir of Thos.
Wolrich of Alconbury, co. Huntingdon, esquire) who was married
1572 and died 1594. Basil Fielding, we remember, was the name
of the famous Earl of Denbigh and Lord of Newnham Paddocks
who distinguished himself so much in the Parliamentary Army in
the great civil wars of the days of Charles the First.—(*Merchant's
bks., Ducat. Leod.* 208., *Vicars' Worthies.*)

[j] Thoresby, under 6 May, 1682, mentions "taking leave of
Alderman Jackson, of Carlisle, which lost most of the forenoon."

she parted with her religious mother, Margaret, Countess Dowager of Cumberland, to Appleby, a well-built pretty town, with a stately castle, rebuilt by the said noted Countess, who, with her mother, the said pious lady, lie entombed under two stately monuments; thence by some country towns, amongst the hills, to Kendal, the chief town in Westmore_ land. 24. Viewing the town and church, transcribing some monuments of the Bellinghams, Stricklands, Judge Nichols, &c.; thence by Kirby Lonsdale, so called from the river Lune, that runs by it, over the Moors, &c. to Giggleswick."

In November, 1682, he again entered our bounds, in company with Mr. Richard Mann: after mentioning that in the church at Catterick are "several curious large blue stones with statues in brass, and inscriptions as old as 1412, for the Burghs, of Burgh, hard by; where now inhabits Sir John Lawson, whose lady,[k] and Lady Braithwait, are here interred, but without any inscription," he says "8. From Catterick we rid to Piercebridge, an ancient Roman colony, where have been dug up many of their coins and inscriptions, particularly that altar I have at home. It is now a poor village, without either church or chapel. Thence, by Walworth-hall, a

[k] Descended from the Lawsons of Northumberland and Durham.

delicate seat of the Jenisons, built archwise with
turrets. Thence, by Highinton and Elden, to Kirk-
marinton, the church whereof is built upon so high a
hill that it is seen many miles off. There, had a
prospect of Durham Abbey, whither (leaving Brans-
prth Castle, the delicately pleasant seat of the ingenious Sir Ralph Cole, on the left hand) we arrived
in time to observe the antiquities of St. Cuthbert
and his Cow (cut in stone upon the Minster,) and
venerable Bede, who lies interred under a stately
blue marble, but without inscription save this, hand-
somely chalked round the edge, *Hâc sunt in fossâ
Bedœ venerabilis ossa.* Observed too, the Castle and
Bishop's Palace, much built and beautified by the
memorable Bishops Tonstal and Cousins, who built
also the alms-houses in the Square, and the' Library,
as appears by the arms fixed upon them in many
eminent places. Viewed also the Tolbooth and
Cross, built by ditto Tonstal; and spent much of
the evening with Cousin Mich. Walker's. 9. Morning, rode to Chester, and stayed with Aunt Thoresby and cousins. Wrote some of the inscriptions of
the tombs of the Lords Lumley, from Lyulph the
first, who flourished in King William the Conqueror's
time, and was a great cherisher of St. Cuthbert;
whose ancient monuments scattered in the neigh-
bouring abbeys, and at Durham, were collected and

placed there in a curious delicate manner, by John, ninth lord. Thence, got well to Newcastle; spent the evening in business, viewing the town, &c.

10. Up very early, and having dispatched business, rode with ditto Mr. Richard Mann to North Shields. By the way had a sight of a pleasant hall of Mr. Clark's, now Captain Bickerstaff's.[1] Went to view Clifford Fort; copied the inscription. It is fortified with forty cannons. Had a prospect of Tinmouth Castle, and ancient church; and below, of the Spanish fort, built close by the sea by Queen Elizabeth. After having observed their way of boiling salt, ferried over to South Shields. Thence, through Weston, and within sight of Whitburn, by

[1] In 1672, one of the auditors of the family of Percy, named Joseph Clarke, obtained of the Countess of Northumberland a gift of the materials of Warkworth Castle, in order that he might build himself a house at Chirton, near North Shields; and he accordingly unroofed the keep, for the sake of the timber and lead. Chatto remarking on this enormous proceeding, says, "what other injury the building might sustain through the cupidity of this *honest* steward, who had obtained from the youthful countess permission to dismantle the castle of her ancestors, in order to build himself a sty—does not appear: the walls were probably spared because he had found that it would be more expensive to pull them down, and separate the stone from the hardened lime, than to purchase new stones from the quarry."

Philip Bickerstaffe was a free burgess of Newcastle, a member of one of the twelve mysteries of the same town, and was admitted to his personal freedom of the fellowship of Hostmen, 11 Sept. 1684. He occurs acting a justice of the peace at his house in Chirton from 12 Jan. 1683, and probably earlier.—(*Grose Ant., Chatto Rambles., Session pprs. Nd., Hostmen's bks.*)

the sea to Hilton, the seat of an ancient family of
that name; whereof Baronet Hilton (as the report
is, from some private dissatisfaction because of his
marriage with an inferior woman, which put him
upon a resolution that none from her should heir
above 100*l.* per annum) gave the ancient estate
(being about 3000*l.* per annum) to charitable uses,
making the Lord Mayor of London and Aldermen
trustees, for the term of one hundred or else one
thousand years, wanting one.™ Thence, by Cleden

™ Henry Hilton, baron Hilton, son and heir, was a child at the
death of his father, and was in ward to her majesty, and by indenture between the queen and Thomas Marbury: it was covenanted
that he should bring the said Henry, when he was ten years of age,
to the bishop of Carlisle to be reviewed and talked with "that his
manners, education and profitting in learning may be understanded
and perceaved, upon payne of forfature of the said warde." Little
further is known of Henry, except that he lived much at Michel
Grove, in the county of Sussex, and was a melancholy man, and
that he nearly ruined his family by his improvident and posthu-
mous generosity. He appears to have been so much under the in-
fluence both of vanity and melancholy, as might in these days of
equity, have occasioned serious doubts as to the sanity of his dis-
posing mind. He married Mary, daughter of Sir Richard Wortley
(who remarried sir William Smith). He died on the 30 March,
1641.

By his will, dated 26 Feb. 1640-1, he devised the whole of his
paternal estate for ninety-nine years to the lord Mayor and four
senior aldermen of London, on trust to pay during the same term
£24 yearly to 38 several parishes or townships in various counties,
and an annuity of £100 to his next brother Robert and his heirs,
&c: the residue he gives to the city of London to bind out children
of his own kindred, &c.

The litigations of sir Thomas Smith with the city chamber,
though they tore the estate in pieces whilst the heir starved, had

and Fulwell, to Monck-Wearmouth, where Sir
Thomas Williamson has a pleasant house and gardens. Thence ferried over to Sunderland, where we
lodged. 11. Having overnight observed what was
remarkable in Sunderland, which is of late grown to
a considerable repute and resource for coals and
salt, rode through Bishops-Wearmouth ; which was,
saith Camden, much beautified with chapels by Be-
nedict Bischop, who first procured masons and gla-
ziers in England." Thence, through some country
towns, Easington, &c. to Hartinpoole, where transcribed some things from the ancient church, now
much ruined, as all the town, which has been of
great repute and circumference, as appears by the
large walls, &c. and two very old monuments, to the
full proportion of a knight and his lady, in the
church-yard, and a large marble over the ancient
vault for the . . . . . . It now consists mostly of

eventually a favourable effect. The citizens of London, who derived very little benefit from the will of their singular benefactor,
were wearied out with the contest, and after the restoration, an
amicable decree was pronounced, by which the estates were restored
to the heir on condition that he should discharge all the particulars
of the trust created by Henry Hilton. He was unable to satisfy
all demands however, and the payments were reduced in proportion
with the rent roll, leaving still a very sufficient burden to exercise
the prudence and patience of the family, both which useful qualities
they seem to have possessed in a very exemplary degree.

" These circumstances relate to Monk-Wearmouth, not to Bishop-
Wearmouth.

Bishop of Durham, for thirteen poor men, who have
40s. per annum, and have an old chapel for Beads-
men's prayers. Thence to Billingham, the ale whereof is noted in Northumberland, Durham, &c. ;
through Norton to Stockton, which has a pretty
Town-house and handsome buildings, but of no anti-
tiquity, but very prettily covered with Dutch tiles.

12. Die Dom. The vicar° (this being only a chapel of ease) preached from Psm. xxxiv. 9, " Fear the
Lord ;" showed prettily how apt we are to fear such
things as are seldom observed, or that appear in an
extraordinary manner as eclipses, lightnings, thun-
ders, &c. which proceed even from natural causes,
and yet how few make them arguments to fear the
shippers, fishers, &c. to the poor whereof ditto Hilton,
Baronet, left 24l. per annum (though now it amounts
not to above 16l.) Thence over the sands to Cre-
tham, where is a very old hospital, built by Robert,

° This we would take to be meant for Thomas Davison, A.M.,
who was collated to the vicarage of Norton, 1663, in which year
being " desirous to gratify the inhabitants of Stockton with a preacher,
Thomas Rudd, gave up his school, and applied himself to preaching,
for which he had an annual salary of £26 and the surplice fees,
and so he continued till 2nd February, 1689, when Mr. Davison
was turned out for refusing to swear allegiance to Wm. and Mary.
Mr. Rudd was made vicar in his place ; yet was so kind to his old
worthy master, as that he freely permitted him to continue in the
vicarage-house, and enjoy all the profits as formerly, he finding a
curate, and only reserving for himself the profits of the chapelry of
Stockton."—(Surtees' Dur.)

Lord, who made the heavens and earth; and then for comets, apparitions, whales, what strange effects they have upon vulgar apprehensions; and then gave a lash or two at the poor Dissenters, if not at serious piety, under the odious name of Presbyterians, full of fears and needless jealousies, and tumultuary petitions; but, saith he, " if we did but aright fear the Lord, we should not need to fear Pope, or French, or Presbyterians." After dinner, I thought to have rode some miles to a sermon, but could not hear of one in the whole country; so went to hear the town minister, after prayers, catechise children, and expound, which I was glad to observe, in a plain, profitable manner, for instructing the vulgar; he was upon the eighth Command, and having before insisted upon the several sorts of stealth, theft, robbery, oppression, sacrilege; and showed well the reason of all this to be from want of content with the state and condition wherein God has set us, and advised very honestly to that great duty, from the danger of the contrary error, which without repentance would ruin the soul, which was worth more than the whole world.   13. Morning up pretty early; ferried over the river at Stockton, and thence to Acklam."

On 17 Sep. 1694, he occurs " preparing for a journey into Cumberland, about sister D. S's. concern,

taking leave of relations; set forwards about ten "
and towards the close of the ensuing day entered
" Kirkby Lonsdale a very pretty well-built market-
town, with a church, &c. which the shortness of the
days and length of the miles prevented our observ-
ance of, more than the bare view as we rode through
the town, where we passed the river Lean, or Lune;
thence over several high hills, where yet we had the
prospect of much higher, to Kendal, eight miles,
where we lodged. 19. Morning, rose pretty early;
went to church before well light, transcribed some
monuments erected since those I formerly noted;
that, especially, of Mr. Sands, a benefactor to this
town, where A. D. 1659, he erected an hospital for
eight poor widows, who have each 12*d.* per week,
besides a salary to a Reader or Schoolmaster, &c.;
which fabric (wherein we saw one widow weaving
their woollen manufacture,) I believe he first designed as a workhouse, by the tazels, &c. cut in stone
upon the front. And this town, which is the chief
in Westmorland, is yet a place of trade, Kendal cot-
tons being famous all England over. It is a handsome well-built town, but cannot pretend to any
great antiquity; and the Castle is ruinous, formerly
the prime seat of the Parrs, where the Lady Cathe-
rine Parr, (the last of King Henry VIII,'s wives,
and a great favourer of the Gospel,) was born, From

Kendal, we rode by Stavely, four miles, to Amble-
side, six (at the end of Winandermere, *prægrande
stagnum*, the most spacious lake in all England, saith
Speed,) now a country vill, but of old, as appears by
the many heaps of rubbish and ruins of walls, as well
as by the paved highways leading thereto, a noted
Roman station—Amboglana, as Camden conjectures.
Thence, over Eyn-bridge, and many high hills,
amongst which the said melancholy river runs, upon
which a remarkable *catadupa*, cataract, or waterfall,
which falling from a great height, and breaking upon
the rugged rocks, affected both the eyes and ears
with somewhat of horror, especially us that were
riding upon the steep and slippery side of the hill;
to Fellfoot, four miles ; and then ascended a dreadful fell indeed, terrible rocks, and seemingly inaccessible ; much more likely for the goats to scramble
over, than horses or men ; especially those two more
notorious of Wren-nose and Hard-knot, which were
really mighty dangerous, terrible, and tedious, and
had nothing to comfort us but the certainty of being
in the right way, for the prodigious rocks on the
right hand, upon that ugly Wrynose were absolutely
inaccessible, and on the left nothing but a ghastly
precipice to the Fell-foot, which I think may as well
be called Hell-foot, as those riverets (which Camden
mentions p. 727) Hell-becks, because creeping in

waste, solitary and unsightly places,[p] amongst the
mountains upon the borders of Lancashire; which,
not distinctly remembering, I mistook several little
becks for, which came rumbling down these high
mountains into valleys, hideous enough in places.
Upon the height of Wrynose, we found the three
shirestones reared up, which bound as many counties, upon two whereof a man may set either foot,
and sitting upon the third, may be at the same time
part in Lancashire, Westmorland, and Cumberland,
which we here entered upon, and walked down the
hill. After which, we rode over several high hills,
but accounted little because of Hard-knot, whose
rugged head surmounted them, upon the top of
which (when not without difficulty we had scaled it)
I was surprised to find the ruins of some castle or
fortifications where I thought the Romans had never
come. Having at length surmounted the difficulties
of these eight miles' tedious march from Fell-foot to
Dale-garth, (which was rendered still more uncomfortable by the loss of a shoe from the servant's
horse, which much retarded our journey,) we came
into a pleasanter country by the river Esk; and
being recommended by Mr. Frankland, visited Justice Stanley at Dalegarth, to enquire after Mr. S.
Thence seven miles good way in a habitable part of

[p] We would rather say from *hel,* meaning water.

the earth, by Gosforth, the pleasant seat of Mr. Copley, to Cauder-bridge, where we arrived safe, though late, in a dark night and strange country, but necessitated thereto for want of conveniences nigher, and here found them very slender ; jannock bread and clap-cakes the best that gold could purchase; but we made ourselves merry with the music of our clog-slippers, and complimented them to entertain us at Bernard Swaneson's whose family he saith has been there 380 years, as Mr. Patrickson, an ingenious gentlemen of Cauder Abbey adjoining, tells him.

20. Morning, enjoyed Esquire Curwen's of Sellay Park, good company, and serious advice (upon Mr. Frankland's recommendation) to decline a Cumberland match, &c. ; in our road from Cauderbridge we had a fair prospect of the Irish sea, to Egremont, three miles, where we saw the vestigia of an ancient castle. Thence by the iron mines, where we saw, them working and got some ore, (which is transported to Ireland where it is smelted) and . . .' where worthy Bishop Grindall was born ; to Whitehaven five miles, where we spent the rest of the day in pursuing directions in quest of Mr. S's. estate;

' Edmund Grindal, archbishop of Canterbury, was born in Hensingham, in the parish of S. Bees, co. Cumb., and died 6 July, 1583. He was the founder of the Grammar-school at S. Bees.—(*Jefferson's Allerd. above Darwent,* 354-5.)

and in viewing the town, which is absolutely the
most growing thriving town in these parts; much
encouraged by Sir John Lowther, the lord thereof,
who gave them four hundred pounds towards building the pier, and two hundred pounds towards the
building of a church, which is one of the prettiest I
have seen, (after the London mode of their new
churches) with the ground that it stands upon; and
he is now building a very stately school-house, to
which he designs the addition of two wings, one for
teaching the mathematics, and the other writing.
We walked thence along the designed Lowther-
street, for it is grown from a village of six houses, as
Major Christian,[r] a native of the Isle of Man, (which
we had the prospect of upon the hills,) and many
others can remember, to a large town, full as big as
Pontefract (even in brother Rayner's judgment), to
Sir John Lowther's stately house at the Flat, where
we were most obligingly entertained by William Gilpin, Esq. (the doctor's son, of Newcastle,)[s] a most
ingenious gentleman, who showed us the pictures

[r] Are we to consider the John Christian mentioned in the following note as the Major Christian of the text? Ewen, son of John
Christian of Millton, Isle of Man, gentleman, apprenticed to Francis
Grey, merchant and adventurer and mercer of Newcastle, 8 July,
1665; set over to Robert Carr to serve the remainder of his time,
4 June, 1669.—(Merchts. bks.)

[s] See post.

E

and curiosities of the house and gardens, wherein is placed the original famous altar, GENIO LOCI, (mentioned by Camden, p. 770,) for which Sir John gave twenty pounds.' This ingenious gentleman, who is an accurate historian and virtuoso, presented me out of his store of natural curiousities, with a very fair piece of Marchesites, and obliged me extremely with his pleasing converse, till pretty late at night with Dr. Jaques and Mr. Anderton, (one of Mr. Frankland's pupils, and the Nonconformist minister there) with much good company, amongst which, honest Mr. Atkinson, the ship-master, who wrote an obliging letter, to recommend us to Mr. Larkham, for further instructions about Mr. Salkeild, though little expectations of success. 21. Morning, rose pretty early; yet prevented of too hasty a journey by the most obliging Mr. Gilpin, who afforded us his acceptable company till we left the town. We rode very pleasantly upon the shore, and had a fair prospect of the Isle of Man, (which peaks up with mountains in

' 'The Flatt' was the manor house built about 1644, by sir John Lowther, discribed by Denton in 1688 as "a stately new pile of building called the Flatt." The present Whitehaven Castle, a seat of the earl of Lonsdale occupies the site. The altar to which Thoresby alludes, was found before 1559 at Ellenborough, and is read "Genio loci Fortunæ reduci Romæ Æternæ et Fato bono Gaius Cornelius Peregrinus Cohortis ex provincia Mauritaniæ Cæsariensis Domos et Ædem Decurionum restituit." On the back of the altar, near the top, is inscribed " Volánti Vivas."—(*Jefferson's Allerd. above Derwent*, 367-8.)

the midst) and part of Scotland, which appears also
vastly mountainous; eastward also, we had the noted
Skiddaw hill on our right hand, which with its high
forked head, Parnasus-like, seems to emulate Scruf-
fel-hill, in Annandale, in Scotland. The Cumber-
landers have a proverb :—

> " If Skiddaw hath a cap,
> Scruffel wots full well of that,"

applied to such who must expect to sympathize in
their neighbour's sufferings by reason of the vicinity
of their habitations ; *Tum tua res agitur paries cum
proximus ardet.* We· rode by the ruins of an old
building, which seemed to have been some religious
house, and through a silly boor's mistake, prevented
of the sight of Workington, a noted market town by
the sea, and turned a worse road over the Moors,
and some slender country vills, Clifton, &c. to Cock-
ermouth; a well built market town, with a church
and castle upon two hills, almost surrounded with
Darwent and Cocker ; it enjoys, also, a good school,
endowed with about thirty pounds per annum, by
the Lord Wharton, &c.; but we saw little, save the
town-house we rode by, designing, though prevented,
to return and lodge there. Having passed Darwent,
I called at Bride Kirk, or St. Bridget's Church, to
see that noble monument of antiquity, the font, with

a Runic inscription, which, even the learned Camden understood not; but is since accurately described by my honoured friend, the reverend and learned Mr. William Nicholson, Archdeacon of Carlisle, in a letter to Sir William Dugdale; Nov. 23, 1685; printed in the Philosophical Transactions of that year; and in another to me, of Sept. 9, 1691, wherein he obliged me with the curious drafts of several Roman monuments found in Cumberland since Mr. Camden's time, and that famous cross at Beaucastle, with the Runic inscription, explained in a letter to Mr. Walker, then Master of University College, in Oxford, 2d November, 1685, printed also in the said Transactions, p. 1287, &c. though in this to me he has added a delicate inscription of nine lines upon the west side of that stately monument, found out, I presume, not only since that communicated by the Lord William Howard to Sir Henry Spelman, and mentioned by Wormius Mon. dan. p. 161; but since that to Mr. Walker, being not exemplified in the said Transactions, as the shorter inscriptions upon the north and south sides are. My said worthy friend, was pleased at the same time to favour me with his notes of my embrio manuscript account of Leeds, and very learned and accurate remarks upon some coins I had transmitted to him, especially upon that Amulet of the old idol Thor, with the Runic inscription, of which, *inter alia*, he writes me ; " I never yet saw any Runic inscription so plain and intelligible, which I hope to find exemplified in the new edition of Camden's Britannia, being engraven (though badly enough, Table II.) with many more that the importunity of the gentlemen concerned prevailed with me to communicate, most of which are returned, with very kind expressions of gratitude, from the said poor (but ingenious) Mr. Ob. Walker and Mr. Edmund Gibson, who published the Saxon Chronicle, my very obliging and kind friends, though yet never seen by me, no more than the glory of my correspondents about antiquity, Mr. Archdeacon, till this journey from Bridkirk, where the honest parson was very obliging in showing us the said famous font and the register, where one of his predecessors had writ a small account of it, but without any knowledge of the letters ; we rode to Talentire to consult Mr. Larkham, the Nonconformist minister, to whom Mr. Atkinson recommended us, (son to a good old Puritan, some of whose works are in print,) about Mr. S. but received the strongest reasons imaginable against it, and not fit to be communicated but to very choice friends concerned ; he walked with us to Mr. Fletcher's Copper Grove, where they are beginning to mine for the mineral ore, which abounds in this county ; thence, after a

consultation, we rode over the Moors, directly to
Threepland, to Esquire Salkeild's, who, being all
abroad at Bothal, &c. about the harvest, we were
under a necessity to comply with them, and thank-
fully accept a night's lodging, though against my in-
clination, because forseeing a rupture, &c.

22. Morning, discoursed the old gentlemen about
the terms; and after, walked to view part of the
land; and, by their excessive importunity and pretence of business in giving particulars of estate, prevailed with to stay till Monday; spent. part of the
day in coursing with the young gentleman, while
the old Esquire was preparing a rental, and in visiting honest Parson Robinson, of Plumland; after,
had Mr. Orphir's company; evening, discoursed Mr.
Salkeild, sen. again about ditto concern. 23. Die
Dom, it should be; though, alas! some part
little like it, no prayers of any sort in family; we
walked to Plumland, where worthy Mr. Robinson
prayed and preached very affectionately and wel
from Luke x. 42. Doctrine, that nothing is need-
ful comparatively to the salvation of the soul; many
gentlemen invited to dinner, so that rest of day and
evening was spent very unsuitably to the duties of
the day, though we enjoyed the modest parson's
good company, and Esquire Dyke's; evening, sat
too late, or rather early, with the young gentleman,

and was foolishly cheerful, and vain in my expressions; too compliant, &c. 24. Morning, taking
leave of ditto family, who have very obligingly entertained us; of honest Mr. Robinson, Parson
Holms, &c.; then rode by Bold, or Bothal, where
viewed the land and mill, which gave little content;
thence, to Torpenna two miles, their parish church,
where Mr. Archdeacon preacheth; thence, to Ireby,
a market town, three miles, which Camden supposes
to have been that Arbœia, where the Barcarii Tigri-
enses kept their standing guard; thence, by Caud-
bec to Park Gate, three miles; thence, to Heskit
two miles, Newgate one mile, and to Hutton, four
miles, where we viewed Sir George Fletcher's very
stately hall, which is by far the most delicate noble
structure we saw in these parts, (not having time to
see Lowther, where Sir John Lowther is building
such a palace-like fabric, as bears the bell away from
all): thence five miles to Salkeld, the pleasant habitation of my honoured and kind friend, Mr. Archdeacon Nicholson,* whose long-desired society I now

* William Nicholson, afterwards bishop of Carlisle. This celebrated prelate to whose industry and learning the historians of
Cumberland are so deeply indebted, was the son of the Rev. Joseph
Nicholson, rector of Orton, near Carlisle, at which village he was born
about 1655. He was elected to the see of Carlisle, 1704, translated
to Londonderry, 1713, and elevated to the Archbishopric of Cashell
in Feb. 1726, but he died suddenly on the 14th of that month,
and was buried in the cathedral of Londonderry without a monument—except that sufficient one raised by himself in his historical
and literary labours.

enjoyed with great delight. We presently retired
from the company to his museum, where he showed
me his delicate collection of natural curiosities, (and
very kindly bestowed several of them upon me,) some
coins and medals, but the earth in those parts, where
most have been found, being of a very corroding
nature, many of them are extremely eaten; many
choice authors in print, but, above all, I was most
pleased, with his own most excellent manuscripts,
especially his manuscript history of the ancient kingdom of Northumberland, in two volumes, in Latin
folio, which yet put me to the blush; looking in the
Villare for what remarks he had procured concerning Leeds, I, altogether unexpectedly, found my
name inserted with titles far above me, for the ety-
mology of the name, &c. We after walked to see
the town, and river Eden, which rumbles not as most
in Cumberland, whose courses are much obstructed
with rocks and stones, but runs sweetly by the town,
which is, without compare, absolutely the pleasant-
est country town we have seen in these parts of
England; but we had not time to visit Long Meg
and her daughters at the less Salkeld, longing to be
again in that little paradise, his study, &c. After
supper, he showed us several remarkable sea-plants,
and obliged us with most excellent converse, that I
almost grudged my sleeping time.

25. Morning, rose early, to enjoy Mr. Archdeacon's most acceptable converse and papers, which were the most pleasing and instructive that I could tell how to wish for; after, took leave of his modest good lady and family, but enjoyed his excellent company ten miles to Appleby, in the way whither, he showed us an old Roman camp, and the ruins of Gallatum, of which, *vide* Camden, p. 761. At Appleby, (the Roman Abbalaba, where the Aurelian Maures kept a station,) we were very nobly entertained with much good company at a venison feast, at the Rev. Mr. Banks', the head schoolmaster there, whose learned company, with that of the nonesuch Mr. Nicholson, was extremely obliging; he showed us the school and library, and a most curious collection of Roman inscriptions on the walls of an adjoining garden-house, placed there by the learned Mr. Reginald Bainbridge, whom Mr. Camden and Sir Robert Cotton celebrate, as the excellent master of the school, when they made their survey of these parts; the late learned Bishop Barlow, of Lincoln, and this present Bishop Smith, of Carlisle, (who is now building a public edifice upon pillars and arches, for the use and ornament of the town,) have been considerable benefactors, &c. The late worthy Bishop Rainbow's life is writ, and published by the said ingenious Mr. Banks, who has also printed

other things. After much pleasing converse, (wherein I had abundant reason to admire, as the inge-
nuity, so the candour also, of these learned persons,
in taking notice of so insignificant a being, &c.) I
left this ancient and pleasant town, and most excellent company, which I was so enamoured with, that
I would not spare time to view the church, castle, or
hospital, of which, *vide* my former journey into these
parts, thirteen years since this very month, &c., and
rode by Warcup, four miles off, to Brough, for distinction called Market Brough, where lodged, but
walked to the Castle Burgh, to see the church, which
had a good ring of bells, but no monuments, except
we reckon the old-fashioned stone pulpit one, and the
painted glass in the windows, which remain the most
entire of any I have seen, having the entire pictures
of many saints, &c. with inscriptions, *ave gratia
plena ;* but I was sorry to find the castle so ruinous,
as is also that at Brougham, yet dare hardly entertain so much as a harsh thought of the Earl of
Thanet, because I hear so great a character of his
charity to the poor, in sending both books, apparel,
and considerable sums of money to the poor, and
less able inhabitants of many towns, and that with
so becoming a privacy, that they scarce know their
benefactor, and knew not what inducements he
might have totally to demolish Pendragon Castle,

which the late memorable Countess of Pembroke
had so lately built from the ground, three hundred
and twenty years after the invading Scots had wasted
it, &c., being one of the six castles, which, with seven
churches or chapels, and two hospitals, that noble
Countess either built from the ground, or consider-
ably repaired, for the good of the country, and the
praise of her well-deserving name.* 26. Morning,

* The lady Anne Clifford was born 30 Jan. 1590, at Skipton
Castle, in Yorkshire, and educated by Samuel Daniel, the historian,
poet laureat, and successor to Spenser. She was the only surviving
child and heir of the gallant and chivalric George Clifford, K.G.
third Earl of Cumberland, by his wife the lady Margaret, youngest
daughter of Francis Russel second Earl of Bedford. She married,
1609, Richard, Lord Buckhurst, afterwards Earl of Dorset, by whom
she had issue two daughters, Margaret, married to John Tufton,
second Earl of Thanet; and Isabella, who was married to James
Compton, Earl of Northampton. The issue of the latter failed in
1678. The Earl of Dorset died in 1624, and in 1630, the countess
married Philip Herbert, Earl of Pembroke and Montgomery, who is
represented to have been very vicious and dissolute, and whose conduct to his wife during the latter part of his life became so unbear-
able that the countess was compelled to leave him. Their issue
died in infancy, and in 1650 she was again left a widow with ample
possessions, and resolving to spend the rest of her days on her property in the north of England, she resorted thither. Here she devoted herself to acts of piety and benevolence, and though she was
then upwards of sixty years old, she immediately set about the repair of the ruins of her castles and the churches. Rainbow remarks
in his sermon preached at her interment, that "she rebuilt, or by
repairing, restored, six houses of her own, but of God's houses, seven."
She also built and liberally endowed in Appleby, an hospital for
thirteen widows. She reared also in Westmoreland a stately obe-
lisk, the remains of which, on the Roman road called the Maiden
way, are still identified by the name of "Countess Pillar," to mark
the spot where, for the last time, she parted with her mother,
Margaret, Countess Dowager of Cumberland, on 2 Ap. 1616, in
memory whereof, also, she left an annuity of 4l. to be distributed

rose early, (having rested badly,) and left this ancient town, the Roman Verteræ, where, in the declining state of the Empire, a captain made his abode with a band of the Directores, and before daylight entered upon the noted Stane-(or stony) more, but got so severe a cold as much indisposed me, with pain and numbness upon the right side of my head, which rendered my journey very uncomfortable. We rode for many miles upon the famous Roman highway, (as also yesterday,) which was here well-paved, by the notorious Spittle on Stanemore, which, though an ordinary inn, yet often most welcome to the weary traveller in this solitary country, which, for twelve miles, has but one other house (Baitings) for the reception of distressed wayfaring persons. About a mile thence, we passed by the noted Rerecross, or Reicross, as the Scots call it, (Roi-cross rather, or the King's-cross,) which their Hector Boetius would have a mere-stone, confining England and Scotland, erected when the Norman William granted Cumberland to the Scots, to hold it as his tenants.* It

to the poor of the parish of Brougham, every second day of April for ever. She died at Brougham Castle, 22 March, 1675, aged 85. —*(Jefferson's Rainbow's Sermon.)*

* It is somewhat curious that Samson Erdeswicke tells us, 1574, that "to the more called Stanymore, the Skotts in tymes past did challeng as theyres to the cross called Rei-cross, in Stanymore. Stanymore is xiij myle over, now inhabited, but xxx yeres past there was onely one howse called *the Spyttal howse, an ynne.*"— *(Harl. MSS. 473.)*

is yet indeed a bounder, but of two counties, West-moreland and Yorkshire, which we here entered upon; and about six miles thence, came to Bowes, a small country town, where we saw the ruins of a small castle, formerly belonging to the Earls of Rich-mond, who had here a thorough toll and furcas, or power to hang: it was a place of eminency in the Roman time,* the first cohort of the Thracians lying here in garrison in Severus's time; and in the de-clining state of the Empire, the band of Explora-tores kept their station at the same Lavatræ, (or Levatræ; for so its ancient name, in the Itinerary,) which being burnt, the succeeding vill was named Bowes by the Britains, with whom, at this day, a burnt thing is called *boath*, *vid*. Camden's Brit. p. 732. From Bowes, four miles to Greta Bridge; in the road, we had a very fair prospect of Barnard Castle, built, and so called by Bernard Baliol, great-grandfather's father of John Baliol, King of Scots, now chiefly famous for bridles there made:ʸ at

* As an illustration of this statement, our good friend Mr. M. A. Denham of Piersbridge, supplies us with the following old saw, still popular in that neighbourhood:

"When Julius Cæsar was a king,
Bowes Castle was a famous thing."

ʸ We also find Staindrop and Boroughbridge to have been noted for the manufacture of sadlery wares: 30 May, 1594, the sadlers of Newcastle enact that none of the brethren "shall b[u]y any Burra-bridge warres that cummes to this towne to be sold in grosse, that is to saye, not above in gyrthe webe ether wovne or harden, not to by

Greta, we baited to inquire of Roman coins, but
found none worth the notice, though of late years
there was dug up a stately piece of Roman gold,
which, by the description, seems to have been in the
declining state of the Empire, in the midst of the
moat (as they call it,) behind the house, which has
been a fair Roman camp, double trenched. Upon
the bridge was the coat of arms of the warlike family
of the Bowes', as I suppose, being three bows, &c.*

above iiij dussene." We also find "a rememberrance that John Foster
bouche [i. e. bought] a serten reade brydelle of a man of Standroppe
the 18 day of Dec. 1594." However jealous of the preservation of
their own rights, the sadlers of Newcastle appear to have been very
regardless of the privileges of others, for at least so early as the beginning of the last century, they occur visiting Boroughbridge fair in
a body, carrying with them a stock of their wares for sale to the
buyers of horses ; and so important had this feature of their trade
become to them, that in 1710, the head meeting-day falling on the
same day as that on which the fair was to be held, they altered it
to afford the brethren an opportunity of attending the sale as usual.
—(Sadlers' bks.)

* It is observable that throughout the account of his visit to
Cumberland, Thoresby has made much use of Fuller's Worthies, and
in many cases transcribed whole phrases. The following detached
passages in Thoresby's diary relate to the object of his visit : 30 June
1694 "sent for by mother Sykes, to consult about a Cumberland
gentleman (Mr. Salkeild), that would court sister D. S. ; discoursed
him seriously and plainly." 10 Aug. "had visitants, relations and
Esquire Salkeild, with recommendation from the Archdeacon of
Carlisle, as to courtship." 15 Aug. "evening, with Parson Robinson, (the Archdeacon's neighbour and friend,) about Mr. Salkeld's
courtship. 16. So this morning received a visit from ditto Cumberland parson, and Mr. Salkeld, after sight of collections, discoursed of
ditto affair ; then, with brother Rayner about ditto concern. Evening, again at Mill Hill, about ditto weighty affair, seriously dis-
coursing sister D. S. about it. By these affairs much straitened in
time, and much more in affections, that I little thought upon the
mispence of so much precious time as I have unprofitably consumed,
being this day thirty-six years of age."

·In May, 1703, Thoresby in company with Alderman Milner of Leeds, visited the north for the last
time, for having in this or the following year retired
from business with a small competency, and his relatives and friends in Newcastle being mostly dead or
removed, he had neither the ties of interest or of
friendship to lead him thither. He and his friend began their journey on the 17th of the month, when he
mentions passing over the site of the forest of Knaresborough, which, says he, " was once so woody, that
I have heard of an old writing, said to be preserved
in the chest at Knaresborough church, which obliged
them to cut cut down so much yearly as to make a
convenient passage for the wool-carriers^a from Newcastle to Leeds, &c. Now, it is so naked that there
is not so much as one left for a way mark, such a
consumption did the blasts make, of which I have
seen great heaps of slag or cinders, overgrown with
moss, &c. now often dug into for mending the highways." 18. "Went to view the town of North
Allerton: found an hospital, called the Earl of Car-

* The Merchants Adventurers of Newcastle, 28 June 29 Hen. viij
enact that "no manne beynge fre of the felloschep shalle by ne
wolle within the buschebreke of Dorame of non of thaym thatt des
by it and to selle it agayn, and thatt non of thys hus schall by no
skynes of no glowers within the busebreyke, non town hecseptyd
but Rechmont towne, and Rechmont schiere, vponne payn of xlb.
to the howes and xxs. to the presentere as h... as it schalle be
proved, as wylle Norththomarland as Busebreke of Dorome."—
(*Merchant's Bks.*)

lisle's, but was the benefaction of another family they matched into, and is only paid by them : it is for four persons, who have each fifty shillings per annum. From North Allerton, we passed by several country villages, but of no great consideration, till we passed the river Tees, in a fruitful country, which produces very large sheep ; we stayed little in Darlington, hasting to Durham, where I found myself under a great disappointment, the ingenious Sir George Wheeler[b] being at London, and also the Bishop ; but, after the prayers, we were very kindly received by the most obliging Dr. Smith,[c] one of the

[b] Sir George Wheler, D.D., prebendary of the second stall in Durham Cathedral, 1684, and rector of Houghton-le-Spring, 1708, being then vicar of Basingstoke in Hants. At Houghton he re-enacted the hospitalities and charitable acts of Barnard Gilpin his predecessor in the place. He died at Durham, 18 Jan. 1723, and was buried in the Gallilee of Durham Cathedral, where a monument was erected to his memory by his only surviving son Granville Wheler.

[c] John Smith, D.D., the learned editor of Bede. On 27 Nov. 1703, he writes from Durham to Thoresby then at Leeds :—

" SIR,—Your haste in passing through Durham was such that I had not time to enter into conversation with you. But you must not think to escape me so. I have some questions to ask you about the manuscript of Bede's History which I understand you have. Pray, Sir, what age do you take it to be of? What place or person did it originally belong to ? Have you the collation of it with any printed edition ? Would you be so kind as send me the account of these, or any other particulars that you know most remarkable about it, I should take it for a favour. And if you would add a specimen of the hand, (if you please in the 4th canon of the Council of Hertford, l. iv. c. 5,) it would be a great satisfaction to me. Whilst I am writing this to you, that I may not send you nothing,) it comes into my mind to remark to you a mistake in your letter to the Royal Society, about the Roman vestigia near your town. The anonymous geographer's book was not printed at Ravenna, but he himself was born there. He is called the Geographus Ravennas, but the book was printed at Paris ; and, as I take it, the place is not Pampocatia but Pampocalia. I was glad to find that my brother was known to you ; your friendship will be serviceable to him, and most acceptable to me. If you see him shortly, pray tell him it is long since I heard from him, and that he is a letter in my debt. Begging heartily your pardon for this trouble, I rest, sir, your assured friend and humble servant,   JOHN SMITH.

prebends of that church, who was concerned for the
Bishopric, in the late edition of the Britannia, who
showed me some original MSS. of that great benefactor, Bishop Cousins; but we had not time to view
the famous collection of the charters of the Scots'
kings, which the Bishop of Carlisle wrote me were
the fairest that ever he saw, the seals very entire, &c.
At Chester-in-the-Street we called to visit our good
old aunt Thoresby, (Alderman Paul Thoresby's
widow,) who is about ninety years of age, yet her
memory and other senses very perfect, and she discoursed piously and prudently, though at present with
difficulty, because of her present weakness.[d] In this

The doctor was prebendary of Durham, 1695, and rector of Bish-
opwearmouth, 1712. He is interred in S. John's College Chapel,
Cambridge. His father was William Smith, M.A., rector of Lowther, in Westmoreland, who had a family of nine sons and one
daughter by his wife Elizabeth daur. of Roland Wetherell of Stockton, niece to sir George Marwood. The doctor's grandfather was
Mathew Smith of Knaresbrough in the county of York.—(*Thoresb.
Corresp. iv.* 39., *Ducatus,* 24., *Surtees' Dur.*)

[d] Paul Thoresby, a merchant and alderman of Leeds, died 1673,
and was the son of George Thoresby of West Cottingwith, co. Ebor.
which George was son to Ralph Thoresby of Woolhouse, near Barnard Castle. Paul married Ann, daur. of John Belton of Rawcliffe;
she died in 1703, aged 90. Joshua Thoresby, son of Paul and Ann,
was of Chester-le-Street, and married Mary, sister of George Lumley,
an artist of great talent. Thoresby displays a pardonable vanity
in the excellent connections of his family, and frequently adverts
to them: under 12 July, 1703, he describes himself to have been
visited by Joshua, at Leeds—" then showing collections to cousin
Thoresby, of Chester-in-the-street, and his wife, of the ancient family of the Lumleys; the second match into that family, John
Thoresby (the younger brother of Christopher, from whom we are
descended,) marrying Margaret, daughter to the Lord Lumley, in

church, I formerly saw the monuments of the Lords
Lumley, of Lumley Castle, in this neighbourhood, but
had not time now ; they are descended from Liulphus,
a nobleman temp. R. Edwardi Confessoris : the present heir was, by King William III., made Earl of
Scarborough. From Chester, over the Fells, which
were so high, and the clouds so low, (an ugly Scotch
thick fog,) that we seemed to be enveloped there-
with ; but, blessed be God, we got well to our
journey's end, but too late to do any business that
night.

19. To inquire for Mr. John Cay, brother to my
late ingenious friend and kind benefactor, Dr. Jabez
Cay,* whose death was a public loss, as well as to me

Henry the Seventh's time." On 23 July, 1703, he was at York, and
while there took an opportunity " to visit the ingenious Mr. Lumley,
(brother-in-law to my cousin Thoresby, of Chester,) an excellent artist in many respects, paints excellently, japans incomparably, and,
what I was most pleased with, works mezzotinto plates very fine,
he made me a kind present of the lady Fenwick's, Dean Combers',
and Czar of Muscovy's pictures, of his own doing."

* Jabez and John Cay were both sons of Robert Key of Newcastle,
a substantial burgess of Newcastle, and a member of the fraternity
of Bakers and Brewers there. Jabez was an M.D. of Padua, and in
correspondence with a great number of the literary and scientific
men of his time, and is especially noted by Thoresby as his " kind
friend and benefactor to his collection of natural curiosities. Sense
and seriousness filled his last hours, as Mr. Bradbury's expression
was. He died 22d January [1702-3.]" John Cay purchased North
Charlton, co. Northd. and gave the family territorial rank. Since this
time they have been chiefly seated in Scotland, and have there
filled the highest legal posts. Among the members of this distinguished family are to be found the present John Cay, esq. of
Edinburgh, F.R.S.E. sheriff of Linlithgow, and member of the Gene-

in particular.   Then to visit good Mrs. Manlove,
(who gave me some original papers of the late Doctor's) to her brother Bennet ; and after, to visit the
widows of Dr. Gilpin,/ (the pious author of Dæmono-

ral Prison Board of Scotland, John Cay, Judge of the Marshalsea,
Robert Hodgson Cay, one of the Judges of the Supreme Consistorial
Court of Scotland, Judge Admiral of Scotland, and L.L.D. of Edinburgh; and last, not least, Robert Cay, the originator of the Newcastle Infirmary.—(Bakers' and Brewers' Bks.; Cay MS., &c.)

/ Dr. Gilpin, at the restoration, was offered the bishopric of Carlisle ; but not being satisfied as to the authority of episcopal government, he, with great integrity and contempt of the world, declined
this high preferment ; and, on the Act of Uniformity, being ejected
from his living, he settled in Newcastle, where he practised physic
with such reputation and success, that his biographer says, "all
necessary means were scarcely thought to have been used, if he had
not been consulted." By his practice as a physician, he realized
considerable property.   During the operation of the penal laws
against Nonconformists, it was proposed to banish the Doctor from
Newcastle ; but Barnes, by persuading the magistrates of his use-
fulness as a physician, procured him quietness to the end of the
reign of Charles II.   His degree of M.D. was taken at Leyden.   He
appears also to have been acquainted with philosophy and chemistry.
He was an excellent preacher, and eminently cheerful, affable, and
prudent.   His conciliatory conduct was exemplified "in keeping
together a numerous congregation, of very different opinions and
tempers."   His principal work is a large quarto volume on Satan's
Temptations.   He claimed to be of Bernard Gilpin's line, and had
his scutcheon pinned on his coffin.   The Doctor's living was Grey-
stoke in Cumberland.—(Life of Barnes', Jefferson, &c.)

Dr. Timothy Manlove was a very promising young minister.
He died 3 Aug. 1699, aged 37 years.   He wrote a treatise on the
Immortality of the Soul, which excited some attention.   He was
minister at Durham, and afterwards at Mill-Hill, Leeds.   While at
Newcastle, he appears to have assisted Dr. Gilpin in his ministra-
tions at the chapel without the Close-gate.   He was buried at S.
Nicholas', 6 Aug. 1699.   Mrs. Manlove, whom Thoresby on 17 Oct.
1694, designates as the doctor's "modest wife," was buried in the
same church, 1 March, 1714.   The doctor, like Gilpin and many
others of his brethren at this period, appears also to have practised

logia Sacra, &c.), and his son-in-law, Dr. Cay; then visited Madam Clavering, daughter and co-heir of the late Esquire Hardwick, of Potter Newton Hall, parochiâ de Leeds; she was very obliging and ingenious, but the pedigree which I designed to transcribe was at their country seat. Afterwards, cousin Milner and I went to see the town-house upon the

as a physician, for we find him, Sunday, 16 Dec. 1694, prescribing to Ralph Thoresby's wife " *inter alia*, the Jesuit's bark, which seemed to do her much good." Thoresby, however, who appears to have been chiefly instrumental in bringing him to Leeds, received but little thanks for the interest he took in his preaching and pecuniary reward—" no little time was spent in collecting, and receiving what others also had collected, and paying it to Dr. Manlove; yet instead of thanks for my pains and charge, was frowned upon, and downright told, except a greater stipend was advanced (which I and a few more were constrained to advance besides our usual quantum) else he threatened to leave the town. He also expressed a particular disgust at my practice in going to hear the Vicar and Mr. Robinson, two excellent preachers, in public, which was a further uneasiness to my spirits." Thoresby afterwards entered the communion of the Church of England.—(*Reg. S. Nich.*, *Brand*, *Thoresb. Diar.*, &c.)

Thomas Bradbury, who was afterwards a celebrated preacher in London, seems also to have assisted Dr. Gilpin. Thomas Sanderson, gent. of Hedley-hope, co. Dur. by codicil, dated 14 Sep. 1704, leaves 10*l.* to the poor of that church which did late belong to the pious Dr. Gilpin; and to Mr. Gill, Mr. Bennett, and Mr. Bradbury, 1*l.* 1*s.* each (will proved 1706.) Most, if not all of these and other nonconformists, from their eminent talents, exemplary piety, influential connexions, and in some cases, from their opulence, were much respected, and seem to have enjoyed more liberty at Newcastle, under the barbarous and vindictive acts of Charles II., than their brethren in most other places. On this account, the bishop of Durham, in his letter to the mayor and corporation, dated 1668-9, calls this town " the nursery of faction in these northern parts," and threatens them with his " majesty's displeasure," for conniving at the " scandalous and offensive meetings " of those " catterpillers " who refused to conform to the law.

Sandhill, to the building of which Mr. Warmouth⁹ gave 1,200*l.* ; took an account of some other benefactions there and at St. Nicholas's Church ; transcribed some epitaphs there and at another church ; went to visit Mr. Hutchinson,ʰ Parliament-man for Berwick, almost purposely that I might once again see the house where my honoured uncle, George Thoresby, and his virtuous consort, lived exemplarily,

ᵍ This was alderman Henry Warmouth, who by his will, 11 Ap. 1654, gave 1200*l.* towards the building of the projected town-court, which when completed in 1658, cost upwards of 10,000*l.* This most munificent benefactor was sheriff (his father William, being mayor) in 1631, and was appointed mayor on the taking of the town in Oct. 1644, in place of sir John Marlay, who was deposed. An inscription prepared by Trollop the architect, is placed against the inner face of the " Exchange," commemorating the bequest. He is named one of the commission which the Commons, 17 Nov. 1642, resolve to move the Lord General to grant for raising of forces in Northumberland, Durham, Newcastle, and Berwick-upon-Tweed, for the preservation of the peace therein ; and in 1645, being then mayor, was one of the commissioners for Newcastle, and for the county of Durham, for raising the association of the Northern Counties. His father, William Warmouth, an eminent merchant of Newcastle, several times governor of his company ; sheriff 1598, and mayor in 1603, 1611, and 1631. He was married at S. Nicholas, 5 Ap. 1592, to Judith, daur. of William Whittingham, dean of Durham. William's father was Robert Warmouth, likewise a merchant of Newcastle, and son of Richard Warmouth. Robert was apprenticed to Bartram Ord, merchant adventurer, in 1546, and admitted to his freedom in 1553. He married Isabella, daur. of Nicholas Baxter, of the same town.—*(Visitation of* 1615., *Reg. S. Nich., Jour. Ho. Com., Ordnce. of Parlt., Tailors' bks.* &c.)

ʰ Jonathan Hutchinson, esq. who died just before 8 Dec. 1711, being member for Berwick up to the period of his death. He was a merchant of Newcastle, and one of the common-council of that town in 1688.

and died piously.' Cousin Milner went with me to
Mr. Ord's, to pay rent for poor brother Jerry's house ;

' If it had not been for this and other evidences of Ralph
Thoresby's, we would have known little or nothing of the parentage and
date of the birth of George Thoresby who was sheriff in 1657-8, for
the enrolment of his apprenticeship does not appear in the merchant's books at the period when he might have been bound. This
we would take to have been the very crisis of the civil wars, and
can readily account for the neglect, in the hurry and confusion which
reigned over every thing during that destructive season. Ralph
Thoresby informs us that George Thoresby was the son of John
Thoresby of Leeds, merchant and alderman, and was born 13
March, 1629. His elder brother John was the father of the Historian of Leeds. George Thoresby then of All Saints' parish, married 31 Oct. 1654 at the church of S. Nicholas, Isabell Lawson,
widow—probably of Roger Lawson, draper, who was buried 11 Ap.
1654. Thoresby was buried 17 Dec. 1674 ; his wife on 25 Jan.
1676,—both at S. Nicholas, leaving no issue. As we have stated
he was sheriff in 1657-8, which being the year in which the Town
Court was finished, one of the bells was inscribed with his name
and office, but the bell was afterwards removed to the chapel of
S. Ann. As a further memorial of this period of our sheriff's history, his nephew Ralph of Leeds treasured in his museum of curiosities there, " a pair of gloves richly embroidered with raised or
embossed work" which he wore on that occasion, as also, those worn
by his wife.

" My aunt Thoresby," says our historian, " (relict of Alderman
Paul Thoresby) told me a remarkable circumstance concerning my
good uncle, Mr. George Thoresby, of Newcastle, whom she visited
in his last sickness, and hearing his sighs and groans into her lodging, went early into his chamber to condole his bad night. ' No
aunt,' said he, ' it has been a good night, for I hope I have got a
step nearer Heaven. It is better for me to have such weary nights,
to disengage me the more from this transitory world.' A dear
friend of his and my father's, was the holy and mortified Mr. El-
kana Wales, of Pudsey."

There was another George Thursby of Newcastle, merchant, par-
tially cotemporaneous with our sheriff, and with whom there is
some danger of confusion. He was the son of Thomas Thursby of
Brafferton in the county of Durham, yeoman, deceased, and was
apprenticed to William Blackett, merchant adventurer and boothman (i. e. corn merchant) on 1 Aug. 1655. He married Mary Raw-

we walked upon the quay to see the ships laded with corn and other merchandize, the life of the town; after, to see the house built for the Mayors of Newcastle, to keep the mayoralty in;' saw the remains of a noble statue of King James II. part of which is already used for bell-metal, &c.ᵏ After, walked to

lin, 6 Nov. 1666, and had issue Elizabeth, Rebecca, Henry, Mary, and Thomas, 1668-74, all baptized at S. Nicholas. In the same company and vending the same kind of merchandize at an earlier period was Richard Thursbie, who being son of Thomas Thursbie of School Ayclyffe, in the county of Durham, yeoman, was apprenticed to George Cooke, merchant adventurer and boothman, on 1 March, 1625, and on 4 July, 1633, was set over to Thomas Lambert another free brother of the fraternity. He was admitted to his freedom and married it may be said simultaneously, he wedding Rosamond Cooke, on 9 June, 1640. She was buried 9 Aug. 1654, and her husband on 23 Oct. 1656.

The Mr. Ord of the text, was probably John Ord, esq. attorney, who in 1705, founded S. John's School in Newcastle, and was the ancestor to the present William Ord, esq. M.P., for that town.

ʲ The Mansion House in the Close was built in 1692, previous to which time the mayoral residence was held at the private houses of the respective holders of the dignity. Since the passing of the "Reform-bill," the house has been converted into a timber warehouse.

ᵏ This was the statue pulled down at the Revolution in 1688, and which has afforded us a subject for another of our tracts. Charles Townley, esq., writing to Thoresby, 1 June, 1707, says, "Mr. Smith, our ingenious bell-founder, purchased and brought from Newcastle, a large part of that equestrian statue of King James, set up, and afterwards thrown down by the mob, at that time. Here is his face very well wrought and very entire, besides several other parts of his body. Had I money, and a house, and place, none should hinder me from purchasing such a great ornament for a garden. There is nothing of Jacobitism in this : were it of that great r—— Cromwell, I should think it of great value; and I hope Mr. Smith will look upon it, and conserve it as such, till some noble purchaser comes that has money, and will think a good round sum well laid out on what in time to come, if not now, may

the very curious bowling-green, built at a public charge, and where are the best orders kept, as well as made, that ever I observed.[1] Evening, with Alder-

prove a curiosity of the first magnitude." In a like spirit, Henry Gyles of York, the glass painter, writing to our historian, 25 Nov. 1707, says "My nephew S. S. bought the remains of King James's statue in brass at Newcastle, which will be melted down ere long; but I have advised him to save a bust of the head to the paps."— (*Thoresb. Corres. iv. 55. 79.*)

[1] "The Forth" with its "Tavern," both shortly to be numbered with the many removals for the purposes of railway communication. There have been many laboured definitions of the name of this place, but the most reasonable appears to be, that this ground lying as it does, without the circum-muration of the town, is *forth* of the walls, or rather gates of the town. The Forth has probably been in use as a place of recreation from a very early period, and that too, counten-anced by the governing body, both in purse and person : in May, 1561, the mayor and aldermen witness and reward the exertions of the "fellyshyp of a shype [of] Albroughe dansyng in the Fyrthe," and in June, 1566, "a player" is presented with 3s. 4d. "for play-inge with a hobie horse in the Firthe before the maior and his brethren." Archery too, it would seem, has been practised here by the stalwart youths of the town, for in July in the same year, we have a charge "for macking up the buttes in the Fyrthe." In 1657, the Forth and paddock adjoining were leased out at the rent of 20l. per annum, for 21 years, with a clause to permit all the liberties, privileges, and enjoyments, formerly used there : amongst these occur "lawful recreations and drying clothes." About this time, a bowling green and house for the keeper, were made by con-tribution, in part of the Forth ; around which, some time after, a wall was built and trees planted by the corporation. In 1682, there was an order of the same body "to make the Forth-House suitable for entertainment, with a cellar convenient, and a hand-some room," &c. A keeper of the bowling-green was retained till about the middle of the last century. "It was an ancient custom," says Bourne, "for the mayor, aldermen, and sheriff of the town, accompanied by great number of the burgesses to go every year, at the feasts of Easter and Whitsuntide, to the Forth, with the mace, sword, and cap of maintenance carried before the them." Then they unbent the brow of authority, and joined the festive throng. The vast concourse of young people of both sexes, at this place, during

man Fenwick,'" at whose house we lodged, and Mr. Banson,'' an ingenious writing-master, who has lately

the Easter holidays, is undoubtedly the remains of this ancient custom. It was also usual for several of the incorporated companies to resort here on their head meeting days, a custom only laid aside in the earlier part of the last century. On the north side of the bowling-green were a tavern, with a balcony and parapet, supported upon an arcade, whence the spectators calmly smoking their pipes and enjoying their glasses, beheld the sportsmen below.—(*Bourne, Brand, Corporation and Companies' books, &c.*)

'" Nicholas Fenwick was the son of Robert Fenwick, of Brenkley, co. Northd. gentleman, and was apprenticed to Ralph Heron, merchant adventurer and boothman, 20 May, 1648. On 6 Feb. 1655, he was set over to Francis Gray, to serve out the remainder of his apprenticeship. In due time he obtained the franchise, was sheriff in 1678, and filled the civic chair in 1682 and 1697. He appears to have enjoyed a more than ordinary intimacy with sir William Blackett and his wife, and in a letter of his which we have seen, oddly enough, written, as in all probability he spoke, in the dialect of the north. On 18 Feb. 1697, he "refars" sir William to a former letter, and informs him that " Mr. Weatwange is looket vpon to be a dyeinge man and continues very ill," and presents his " most humble sarvice" to his "good lady, not forgetting [him]selfe." He was also a coal owner, and admitted to the freedom of the Hostmen by reason of his being a member of one of the mysteries, and as such entitled to the franchise of that fraternity, under the charter of James the First.—(*Merchants' and Hostmens' books, Robinson letters.*)

" William Banson, the ingenious caligrapher, appears to have been appointed writing-master at the Grammar-school of Queen Elizabeth, in Newcastle, when very young. In 1702 he published his work on penmanship, very beautifully executed by Sturt, displaying all the *hands* then in use. The capitals at the commencement of each page and phrase, possess singular beauty, at a period when elegant writing was much more in use and esteemed than now. The lines are interspersed with the figures of birds and fishes, executed with infinite freedom and elegance. Its size is foolscap long folio, and contains thirty four examples. The title is as follows :— " The Merchant's Penman, a new copy book of the Usual Hands now in Practice by most Book Keepers in Europe. By William Banson, Master of the Feee Writing School in Newcastle upon Tyne." Then follows the dedication " to the Right Worshipful y⁰ Major, Re-

H

printed the Merchant's Penman, or a new copy-book,
&c., who went along with me to Mr. Rudd,* who

corder, Aldermen and Sherif, of the Town and County of Newcastle
upon Tyne, your servant having composed a Small Copy Book for yᵉ
Use and Benefit of yᵉ Freemens Sons belonging to the Free School, of
which your Worships were pleased to make me Master, (almost in
my minority.) I therefore most humbly Dedicate the first Fruits of
my weak Endeavours to yoʳ Worships begging yoʳ Acceptance which
will Encourage yoʳ most Obliged humble Servt. William Banson,
Newcastle. June yᵉ 15 M.D.C.C.II." In accordance with a fashion
then prevalent, the next page bears the following commendatory
lines " upon Mr. Willm. Banson, his accurate Copy Book, the value
of which it must be admitted, is not enhansed by his friend's laboured rhyme :

> The Fam'd Inventor of the Printers Press,
> Had he but seen Such Characters as these,
> Would his own much admired Art contemn,
> Vanquished by you APELLES now remains,
> A Venus each small Letter here contains ;
> Great Praise to Learned Virgils lines are due,
> Each Letter here demands like Fame for you,
> Proceed then happy Book, an Offspring know,
> Which Parent nere shall be as bound to own.
> 'Mongst Skilful Artists, Emulation raise,
> Whilst Author Work, and Work doth Author Praise.

> THO. WESTON, Philo-Calligraph-"

Banson was married at S. John's, Newcastle, on 21 Dec. 1669, to
Margaret Yong. He was succeeded by Henry Banson, who at the
time Bourne wrote, lived in part of the building attached to the
school. After his death, his " curious collection of tulips, hyacinths,
iris's, carnations, auriculas, &c." were disposed of at the Assembly-
House in the Groat-market, in 160 lots, at nine o'clock in the morning."

* Thomas Rudd, M.A., became master of the Grammar School,
and of the Hospital of the Blessed Virgin in Westgate (upon which
the school is engrafted) in 1699, and was the author of ' Syntaxis
in usum scholæ Novocastrensis.' He had removed hither from Durham School, to the mastership of which he returned in 1710. He
was made vicar of S. Oswald's in that city, and collated thence to
Northallerton, and in 1729 to the rectory of Washington, in the
county of Durham, where he died 17 March, 1733. He wrote the
disquisition concerning the true author of the history of the Church
of Durham, attributed by some to Simeon, and by others to Turgot.
It is in Latin, and prefixed to Bedford's edition of that work. Lon-

teaches the Grammar school, an ingenious, modest, and obliging person, (see Dr. Gibson's Preface to the New Britannia) ; rest of evening with ditto Alderman Milner till bed-time.

20. Sent for by Madam Clavering, to see a curious pedigree of the Dudleys, her husband's relations ;[p]

don, 1732, 8vo. It ought not to be omitted, says Brand, to the honour of Rudd's memory, that on his motion and request, backed by the recommendation of Sir Robert Shaftoe, recorder, some valuable editions of the classics were purchased by the Common-Council, for the use of the Grammar-school of Newcastle, 1700.

[p] John Clavering of Chopwell in the Bishoprick, esquire, married firstly Anne, daur. of sir Henry Thomson of York, by whom he had Sarah, who became the second wife of William Earl Cowper, viscount Fordwich, baron Cowper of Wingham in Kent, Lord Keeper of the Great Seal, Lord High Chancellor, &c., and· great-uncle to Cowper the Poet. John Clavering's second wife was the lady mentioned by Thoresby—Elizabeth, daughter and coheir of Thomas Hardwick of Potter Newton, co. Ebor. esquire.—(Surtees, Ducatus.)

The Dudleys of Newcastle and Chopwell "though the heralds do not allow them the Dudley lion of Warwick and Northumberland, double queue, vert," are yet upon very good grounds supposed to be of the self same stock. It is a pity that Thoresby, who describes having inspected "a curious pedigree" of the family, did not afford us some of its contents, seeing that the consecutive links are so loose, particularly as his words induce us to think that it extended further back than the descent allowed by the heralds as being fully proven. John Dudley (the first in their pedigree) described of Newcastle, married a daughter of William Carre—his son "Robert Dudlaye" was apprentice to Sir Robert Brandling, knight, merchant adventurer and draper, of the same town, at the "feast of the natyvyte of our lorde 1564." He became one of the Customers of the port of Newcastle, was sheriff 1586, and mayor in 1602. He married Anne, daughter of Christopher Wood, otherwise Cooke, and was buried 7 May, 1613. His son Ambrose, (a family name of the Earls) was of Chopwell in 1615, and living 5 May, 1626. He married Isabel, daur. of Richard Greenfield of Wooton, co. Bucks. His son and heir Toby, was aged 18 in 1615, and then of Chopwell, esquire : he married Jane, daur. of Sir William Blakis-

took leave of Mr. John Cay and Mrs. Manlove;
took leave also of the place in a sad rainy day, the
people as morose at the loss of so many horse-loads
of money, (the old Earl's of Northumberland, now
Duke of Somerset's, rents,)⁹ as my cousin Milner
returns twice a year, with which we made the best
of our way, (without coming at Durham); and
mightily pleased with some remarkable providence
that have attended this worthy magistrate, who is of
a good family; his grandfather was chief magistrate,
of Leeds, yet begun the world with little, being the

ton of Gibside, knight, and was buried at Ryton, 30 May, 1661.
Jane, his daughter and sole heir married Robert Clavering, who in
right of his wife, became, *of Chopwell.* He was the son of John Clavering of Axwell, and brother of sir James Clavering, baronet, and
was buried 10 Feb. 1675-6. Dudley Clavering, son and heir of this
marriage died s. p., and John Clavering his younger brother, who
was baptised 5 March, 1654-5, succeeded to the estate, and became
the husband of the "Madam Clavering" of the text, who was his
second wife. She died 1704.—*(Surtees, Merchants' bks., &c.)*

⁹. The younger of the daughters of the tenth Earl of Northumberland, the Lady Henrietta Percy, having died whilst an infant, the
elder, the Lady Elizabeth Percy, became sole heiress of her father.
She was married to Charles Seymour, known to history as the proud
Duke of Somerset, and had a large family; of which the eldest surviving son Algernon Seymour, Duke of Somerset by descent, and
Earl of Northumberland, and of Egremont by creation, had, with a
son who died young, a daughter and sole heiress, the Lady Elizabeth Seymour. This lady became the wife of Sir Hugh Smithson,
a Yorkshire baronet, who in consequence of this alliance, assumed
the name of Percy and obtained the Dukedom of Northumberland:
and she transmitted to her grandsons by this marriage, Hugh Percy,
the late, and Algernon, the present, Duke of Northumberland,
the sole lineal representations of the last four Earls of the house of
Percy, together with all which should accompany the living blood
of their princely ancestors.—*(Loc. His. Tab. bk.)*

youngest son; but as the Earl of Cork, who was a younger brother, [son] of a younger brother, used to inscribe on the palaces he built, "God's Providence, mine inheritance;" so may this worthy and pious person, who, with a thankful heart to God, recounted to me (with which my heart was much affected,) the various steps of his growth; the first year he commissions for 5,000*l.*; the second for 10,000*l.*; the third for 15,000*l.*; the fourth for 20 or 25,000*l*; and has now dealt for 80,000. per annum; and as an and as an acknowledgement of his gratitude to the grand Benefactor, he designs to leave a considerable sum to pious uses, &c.; of his carriage during his mayoralty, and extraordinary activity in procuring the Act of Parliament for making the rivers Aire and Calder navigable, see my notes elsewhere. We passed by Sunderland-bridge; from whence, to another bridge, at a little distance two persons rode a course, which was so near run that both jumped with that force upon the bridge, that one of the horses and his rider tumbled down the battlement of the bridge, and fell both down together with the stones, yet received no damage. It is yet discernible how much of the bridge fell, by the difference of the lime in memory of which, there is engraven upon the cope-stone, Sockeld's Leap, 1694. We baited at Ferry upon the Hill, which answers Kirk Merington

(in the other road,) as to its lofty situation, and got
in good time to Darlington; viewed the town, where,
by the encouragement of the late Queen Mary, is
settled the linen manufacture; they make excellent
huckaback and diaper, and some damask, &c. Went
to transcribe what monuments I could find in the
church; was pleased to find there, several young persons met to sing psalms, which they performed very
well, with great variety of tunes, &c., but was concerned to see the adjoining house of the Bishop of
Durham converted into a Quaker's workhouse.
There being a funeral, we had the happy opportunity
of public prayers, which was comfortable. 21. The
river Tees not being fordable by reason of the late
rains, we went about by Croft bridge, where Sir
William Chater has a seat, by which means we had
the convenience of seeing the Hell-kettles, the best
account of which, is in my late kind friend Dr. Jabez
Cay's letter, inserted by Dr. Gibson in the new edition of the Britannia, p. 782. We baited at North
Alverton; thence we rode by Sand Hutton, Topcliffe, &c. to Burrowbridge;" and thence home.

THE HUMBLE

Petition and Appeal

OF

THOMAS CLIFFE

A POOR SHIPWRIGHT, INHABITING AT

Northshields.

Newcastle:
RE-PRINTED BY M. A. RICHARDSON, 44, GREY STREET.
MDCCCXLV.

ADVERTISEMENT.

IN that very singular volume called "England's Grievance discovered in relation to the Coal Trade," this "poor shipwright" is stated to have been a carpenter at North Shields, and that he saved many ships from sinking, at "easie rates," which drew upon him the ire of the free carpenters of Newcastle, whose privileges he invaded. The Mayor protected the carpenters, and sent his serjeants to take Cliffe to prison, and because Cliffe's wife "railed" at them, (which she would naturally do in very becoming language, and good set terms,) they struck her; and the blows ultimately caused her death; they broke her daughter's arm, and in the volume above quoted there is a plate representing to the life, this barbarous assault. Cliffe got a verdict against the Mayor, but he suffered so many vexations in his calling, that his "occupation was gone."

Gardiner had no love for the corporation, and he hated monopolies, therefore his statements must be received with due caution.

The free carpenters asserted their well understood rights, and poor Cliffe having served his time at Ipswich, was naturally considered a foreigner.

The tract is valuable however, as a picture of the times.

The inhabitants of North Shields took part with Cliffe, and the ship masters went still farther, as they state that he is disabled from following the trade " which the Lord called him unto," and then pray for an act of Parliament for his express protection.

Newcastle was then the same bustling place it is at present ; the Quay side was then the resort of its merchants, as it is still, and this locality, rife with the busy hum of men, has been fertile in producing individuals who by diligence in trade, and honest industry, have raised their descendants in no very remote degree, to dignify the peerage, and fill the highest offices of the State.

C. S.

Sunderland, January 22, 1845.

TO THE

Supream Authority

of the Nation, the

C O M M O N S

Affembled in

P A R L I A M E N T;

The Humble

Petition and Appeal

OF

Thomas Cliffe a poor Shipwright, in-
habiting at Northfhields in the County of
Northumberland, feven miles from
Newcastle upon Tyne ;

Sheweth,

 Hat according to the custom of
this Nation, & the Laws made
on that behalf, your Petitioner
was bound Apprentice unto one
Robert Bull of *Ipswich,* in the
County of *Suffolke,* with him to
serve, as an Apprentice, for the
space of eight years, to learn his trade of a Ship-

wright; as by the said Indenture bearing Date, *September* 28. 1617. fully appeareth.

That having accomplished his eight years servitude, and attained to some measure of perfection in his Trade, he expected to have enjoyed Freedom and Protection by the Lawes of the Nation, in the exercise thereof; which prohibits all *Monopolies*, as appears by the Statute of the 21. *James*, chap. 3. and Sir *Edward Cooks* exposition thereupon, in his third Part, *Instituts, Chap. Monopolies*; *fol.* 181, 182, 183. In the beginning of which chapter he saith, it appeareth by the preamble of this act (as a judgment in Parliament) that all Grants of Monopolies are against the ancient and fundamental Laws of this Kingdom, and therefore it is necessary to define what a Monopoly is.

A *M*onopoly (saith he) is an institution, or allowance by the King, by his Grant, Commission, or otherwise to any person or persons, Bodies politique or corporate of or for the sole buying, selling, making, working, or using of any thing, whereby any person or persons, Bodies politique or corporate, are sought to be restrained of any freedom or liberty that they had before, or hindered in their lawful trade. And the said learned Lawyer Sir *Edward Cook* in his Exposition of the 29, & 30. Chapters of *Magna Charta*, is there also very full to the same purpose, as appears, 2 *part Instit. fol.* 47. 62, whose fore-mentioned Expositions are published by two special Orders of yours, dated May 12. 1641. June 3. 1642, for good Law to the Nation, which Orders are recorded at the last end of his 2 *part. Instit.*

But so it is, may it please your Honours, your Petitioner inhabiting at *North Shields*, in the County of *Northumberland*, being about seven miles from *Newcastle*, and there exercising his Trade as afore-said, for the maintenance of himself and family ; (by whose care and ability many Ships have been pre-served, as may appeare by the Petition and certifi-cates of several Ship-masters hereunto annexed) is greatly disturbed, and most unjustly prosecuted (even to the ruine of himself, and many others, whose wellfare depends on his endeavours) by severall persons, Shipwrights of *Newcastle*, who maliciously combined together to deprive your Petitioner of the use of his Trade, that thereby they might engrosse all that employment into their own hands, and ne-cessitate such, as are forced to make use of them, to give them their own rates, thereby to enrich themselves by the ruine and oppression of the poor Marriner, which is all together contrary to Reason and Justice.

That in prosecution of the said Design, the said

Shipwrights, &c. make use of the name and authority of the Mayor and Burgesses of the Town of
Newcastle, in whose name, and on whose behalf, (by
pretense of some Grants, or Ancient Customs given
them by the *K*ings of *England*, against Law and
Reason,) they challenge a jurisdiction, by colour
whereof, they exercise a power to hinder all persons
(not free of their Corporation) to use the Trade of a
Shipwright; by the exercise of which usurped power,
the said Shipwrights, Brewers, and Bakers, have
forced severall poor persons to forsake their habitations and Families, not being able to contest with
them, and committed many barbarous outrages,
more especially in *Aprill* 1646. at which time, your
Petitioner having got a Ship off the Rocks, and
being repairing the breaches thereof; the said Ship-
wrights, and their accomplices, came into the said
Ship, and seized your Petitioners men that were at
work, and carryed them away, but having obtained
a bribe of *ten* shillings, they freed them; but the
next day coming to *North Shields*, they the said
Shipwrights, and their accomplices, murthered your
Petitioners Wife; because she spake against their
unjust practizes.

That your Petitioner caused the said Assassinats to
be Indicted, and had the said Indictment found by

the Grand Jury, but by reason of the prevalency of the then Mayor, and Burgesses of *Newcastle,* he can obtain no justice nor right against them.

That for the further ruine of your Petitioner, they have preferred a large English Bill in the Court of *Exchequer* against him, hoping thereby either to force him to give over his Trade, although he live seven miles from *Newcastle,* or forsake his habitation, or otherwise to undoe him with a chargable Suite, to defend himself against a whole Corporation, who have unjustly and illegally combined against him.

Now forasmuch as he hath served eight years for his Trade, and inhabiteth in a County distinct from *Newcastle,* it being a Town and County of it self, and *North Shields* in the County of *Northumberland,* and for that it cannot be supposed, that the privilege of a single Corporation can legally extend it self into severall Counties, so many miles distant thereby to destroy the interest and property of many persons, as this pretended, unjust privilege of theirs doth. And for that your Petitioner is informed by his Councell, that if any such Grant be, it is altogether illegall, and destructive to the Liberties of *England,* and therefore not valid, or binding, neither ought to be continued, And for that (if the said Grant should take place, or they be suffered to obtain their ends,) Many good Ships which by casualties of wea-

ther, &c. are cast upon the Rocks, &c. must of necessity perish, by reason of the distance from the
mouth of the Harbour, the Port of *Newcastle* being
about eight miles; as also for the other reasons contained in the Petition of severall Masters of Ships
hereunto annexed.

Your Petitioner humbly prayeth:

*That Your Honors will be pleased to declare against
the proceedings of the said Major, and Burgesses
of* Newcastle; *And forasmuch as Your Petitioner
is altogether unable to maintain a Suite in Law
against the said Corporation for defence of his legal
and indubitable Native Freedom, That therefore
Your Honors will be pleased to Order a dismis-
sion of the said Bill, preferred as aforesaid, and
punish them soundly for their Monopolizing In-
croachments and Vsurpations upon the Peoples
Rights, contrary to Law, Reason, and Justice;
and give Your Petitioner, &c. good repairations
for his sufferings and damages sustained by their
illegal Molestations; and this he is emboldened to
pray, because Your Honors were pleased in your
excellent Votes of the 19, & 25, Novemb. 1640. to
Vote all Projectors, Restrainers of Trade, or
Monopolizers whatsoever, or any that now have, or
lately had any share in any Monopoly, or that do
receive, or lately have received any benefit by any*

Monopolies, or have procured any warrant, or command for the restraint or molesting of any that have refused to conform themselves thereunto, upon proof thereof to be disabled to sit or vote as members of your House as men that have no power nor right to sit there

And Your Petitioner shall ever pray, &c.

THOMAS CLIFFE.

To the Right Honorable the Com-, mons affembled in Parliament.

The humble Petition of the Inhabitants of North-sheelds *in the County of* Northumberland, *whose names are subscribed.*

Humbly ſhewing,

Hat *Northsheelds* is scituated in the Mouth of the River of *Tyne,* the *Anchorage* and other Royalties whereof do belong to the right honorable the Earl of *Northumberland,* in the harbour whereof Ships of greatest burden may safely ride, but cannot pass further upon the River to *Newcastle* (which is eight miles distance) without danger, nor return with full loading, but are compelled to have part brought unto them to *North-sheelds* in small Vessels.

That the Masters of Ships have always heretofore made use of the Inhabitants of *Northsheelds* to repair their Ships, and for their other necessary occasions, and (in times of distress) have thereby saved·

their Ships, which, in all probability, would have
been otherwise lost, as appears by Certificate of near
80 persons, who are Masters of Ships, and Traders
to *Newcastle*, ready to be produced.

That the Burgesses and Freemen of *Newcastle* do
dayly vex and trouble your Petitioners with Arrests
and vexatious Suits, which your Petitioners are not
able to undergo, for using their several Trades at
Northsheelds, and do at this present prosecute *Thomas
Cliffe*, a Ship Carpenter of the same, (by whose abil-
ities the said Masters and Traders have received
great benefit, as by their said Certificate is confest,)
and divers others of your Petitioners, who are Smiths,
and other useful Tradesmen in the Chancery and
Court of Exchequer, and do give out speeches, that
they will not permit Bakers, nor any other Tradesmen (save only Freemen of *Newcastle*) to use their
Trades at *Northsheelds* or *Southsheelds* and for that
purpose they have made a common Purse, notwithstanding *Northsheelds & Southsheelds* is not within the
Liberties or Jurisdiction of *Newcastle*.

That the said Burgesses and Freemen being Masters of the Coal Mynes, will not permit any Masters
of Ships to lade with Coals, if they do not first discharge their Ballast upon the Ballast Keys belonging
to themselves, nor will afford them reparations and
necessary supplies, but at their own excessive rates ;

so that if your Petitioners be prevented in using their Trades, that ancient town of *Northsheelds*, which hath been very advantagious to the Publique, will be depopulated, and the free Trade, and Common Good of the whole Kingdom will be much impaired.

Your Petitioners therefore most humbly pray, That the Inhabitants of Newcastle *may be required to appear by their Agent sufficiently authorized, and that the business may receive a full hearing in this most Honorable Parliament, and be regulated, according to Law and Iustice, and as shall be thought fit for the Common Good, and your Petitioners Relief.*

And your Petitioners will duly pray, &c.

Thomas Cliffe.	*Christopher Blunt.*	*Thomas Lamson.*
Iames Hume.	*Thomas Claphamson*	*Henry Atkinson.*
Iames Clark.	*Nicholas Harrison.*	*Iames Beale.*
Will. Collingwood.	*Robert Allison.*	*Iohn Miller.*
Christopher Dawson	*Henry Fenick.*	*Robert Cod.*
Thomas Bavibrig.	*Hugh Lee.*	*Iames Meek.*
Thomas Dowe.	*Cuthbert Wilson.*	*Iohn Hourlstone.*

TO

TO THE

Right Honorable

THE

C O M M O N S

Affembled in

P A R L I A M E N T ;

Humbly sheweth,

Hat we whose names are hereunder written, Master of Ships, and Traders to the Town of *Newcastle*, for the good of the whole Kingdome; having had many disasters at Sea, both by extremitie of weather and otherwise, and dayly such accidents falling out, were forced many times for the safeguard of our Ships, and goods being in distresse, to take the help and assistance of one *Thomas Cliffe*, a very able and sufficient ship-wright, to use his best endeavours for the speedy recovery of our said Ships: without whose help, under God, our Vessels were likely to be lost. But

now so it is, may it please your Honours, that the said *Thomas Cliffe* living at the *North-shields* for his good work, in ayding and assisting us in our extremities, hath of late bin very inhumanely handled, by the Ship-wrights of *Newcastle*, and hath for this divers years by past, bin held in suit of Law by the said Ship-wrights of *Newcastle*, to the utter overthrow, and undoing of himself, his wife and Familie : So that he is disabled to make use of that Trade, which the Lord hath called him unto, and knoweth no other way of relief, but to addresse himself by way of supplication, to this Honourable House of Parliament : he being a very necessary member for the general good of the Kingdom.

> *Therefore, we the said Masters of Ships, being very sensible of the want of such a man, in the time of our extremity : doe most humbly crave, that Your Honours would be pleased to grant an Act, that the said* Thomas Cliff, *or any other man, may have free liberty to use his Calling, & profession as a shipwright at* North-shields, *or* South-sheelds *without the let, or hinderance of the ship-wrights (or any other) in* Newcastle.
> And Your Petitioners as in duty they are bound shall daily pray &c.

Jeremy Low.	Charles Frank.	Samuel Cason.
John Lever.	William Laurence.	Henry Anderson.
William Revely.	Edward Peach.	Edmond Flammond
John Chamberlin.	Benjamin Morsse.	VVilliam Kayse.
Robert Hudson.	Edmond Tye.	Christopher Turner
John Buckenharp.	John Vmfry.	John Corneles.
Andrew Porter.	Henry Fynne.	John Burwood.
Edmond Lever.	John Cole.	Robert Fuller.
Samuel Tye.	Edward Clark.	John VVarkin.
William Wright.	John Dorr.	Richard Stevens.
Robert Lambe.	Nicholas Shevel.	John Borrett.
William Lig.	John Whalle.	Edmond VVright.
Samuel Wiseman.	Nicholas Chapman.	Edmond Cook.
Kobert Sansum.	William Jabee.	John Ghe.
William Ollwer.	George Hill.	Thomas Ruddes.
Robert Keable.	Richard Sewer.	Robert Fulwood.
Henry Creame.	Richard Hukes.	Richard Keebal.
John Tatum.	Edward Paine.	John Eaton.
Stephen Frost.	Richard Foster.	John Moore.
John Warwell.	John Clarke.	John Fasseker.
Thomas Mash.	John Baker.	Iohn Peck.
George Philips.	Goafry Plover.	Iames Hall.
William Lee.	Francis VVillard.	Iohn Morsse.
Robert Kenington.	Hugh Masterman.	Thomas Kenrike.
Francis Wayman.	Mark Hurlock.	

FINIS.

AN

ANSWERE TO THE PROCLAMATION

OF THE

Rebels of the North.

i.e. T. Percy, earl of Northumberland & C. Nevill, earl of Westmoreland

1569.

IMPRINTED AT LONDON BY WILLYAM SERES.
Cum privilegio.

Newcastle:

RE-PRINTED BY M. A. RICHARDSON, 44, GREY STREET.
MDCCCXLIII.

TO

SIR CUTHBERT SHARP,

THESE PAGES

ARE

VERY RESPECTFULLY INSCRIBED

BY

THE EDITOR.

INTRODUCTORY.

HE following curious Ballad* is locally interesting, since it relates to the Rebellion of 1569, in which the principal parties were Thomas Percy, Earl of Northumberland, and Charles Neville, Earl of Westmoreland, for the purpose of liberating the Queen of Scotland, and the restoration of the Roman Catholic Religion.

The first overt act of the Rebels was committed at Durham, where the bibles and prayer books were rent and destroyed; and after a rapid march to Clifford Moor, they mustered all their forces; but unsupported by the Catholics in every other part

---

* In the British Magazine for April, 1833, p. 417, a quotation is given from a churchwarden's accounts, in " 1570, Item, for vij. ballys consarneng ye Rebells, to be soung, vijd." which would tend to the conclusion, that ballads, similar to the present, were published by authority.

of the kingdom, disappointed of promised aid from without, and wanting both talent and money for such an enterprise, they suddenly retreated.—

> " Most shallowly did you these arms commence,
> Fondly brought here, and foolishly sent hence ! "

They then laid seige to Barnard Castle, which was gallantly defended by Sir George Bowes, for ten days ; thus giving time for the Earl of Sussex, lord president of the North, to advance with the forces collected at York, and supported by the army of the South, under the command of the Earl of Warwick.

The rebels, disappointed and disheartened, did not wait to meet the Queen's army, but dispersed and fled on their approach. The Earls and their principal followers took refuge in Scotland. The Earl of Northumberland perished on the scaffold, at York, 22nd August, 1572 ; and the Earl of Westmoreland escaped to Flanders, and passed the remainder of his life in exile, on the slender and precarious bounty of the King of Spain ; and subject to every contumely, discomfort, and privation.—

> " I have lived long enough : my way of life
> Is fall'n into the sear, the yellow leaf ;
> And that which should accompany old age,
> As honor, love, obedience, troops of friends,
> I must not look to have."

He died at Newport, in Flanders, on the 16th of November, 1601.

The immediate subject of this ballad, is a commentary on the first proclamation, issued by the earls of Northumberland and Westmoreland :— viz.

"WE, Thomas, Earl of Northumberland, and Charles, Earl of Westmoreland, the Queen's true and faithful subjects, to all the same of the old Catholick Religion. Know yee, that we, with many other well disposed persons, as well of the Nobility, as others, have promised our faiths in the furtherance of this our good meaning. Forasmuch, as divers disordered and evil disposed persons, about the Queen's Majesty, have by their subtil and crafty dealing to advance themselves, overcome in this our realm the true and catholick religion towards God: and by the same abused the Queen, disordered the Realm, and now lastly, seek and procure the destruction of the Nobility: We therefore have gathered our selves together to resist by force; and the rather by the help of God and you, good People; and to see redress of these things amiss, with restoring of all ancient Customs and Liberties to God's church, and this noble realm: Lest if we should not do it our selves, we might be reformed by strangers, to the great hazzard of the state of this our Country;

whereunto we are all bound."—*Strype's Annals, vol. I. c.* 54, *p.* 547.

In the dispatches of "la Mothe-Fénélon," the French Ambassador, this proclamation is stated to have been signed by Northumberland, Westmorelande, and nine others; and in the "*Apuntamientos para la historia del Rey Don Felipe Segundo de Espana*" it is signed by Tomas, Conde de Nortumberland. El Conde de Vestmorland. Christobal N. Duel. (*Christopher Nevill*). Ricardo Noturn, (*Richard Norton*). Egmundo Rateis, &c. (*Egremond Ratcliffe, &c.*

There are two copies of this black letter metrical tract, (which is of the utmost rarity) at Cambridge: one is in the public library of the University, and the other in the library of St. John's College; and many years ago, a copy was in Longman's Catalogue, which sold at a high price. The Editor is indebted to the kindness of Thomas Wright, esq., M.A., author of "Elizabeth and her Times," (through the courtesy of the author of the Memorials of the Rebellion of 1569) for the present transcript from the first named copy.

M. A. R.

Newcastle, July 19*th,* 1843.

AN ANSWERE TO THE PROCLAMATION OF THE

REBELS OF THE NORTH, 1569.

O LORDE stretch out thy mightye hande
    Against this raging route,
And save our prince, our state and land
    Which they doe go aboute,
For to subvert and overthrowe
    And make this realme a pray,
For other nations here to growe ;
    What so like fooles they say.
You doe imagine (I suppose)
    Yourselves Princes to be
Or else your stile should not be so
    To sende it out with WE.

The princes phrase ye take in hande
    O well disposed men :
A traytor first that worde so spake
    And he that rulde the Pen.

Hir faythfull subiects ye protest
　　Yourselves in wordes to bee,
Bnt marke I pray you how your deedes
　　Doe with your wordes agree.
Can you hir love, and eke obey,
　　As subjectes in their guise,
When you against hir will and minde,
　　With force of armes doe rise.

To all the olde and Catholike
　　That be of such religion
As you be that be franticke madde,
　　And foolish of opinion.
You write that they your minde may know
　　And you their minde againe,
Whether they meane to take your part
　　And so in fielde be slaine
No faithfull man you may be sure
　　Will lyke your crooked style:
Also your trayne if they be wise
　　Will lyke it, but a whyle,

Chorath, Dathan, and Abiram,
　　Or else Achitophell
With Absolon, Adoniah
　　Of their olde faith ye smell.

Indeede your old religion
  Is waxen stale for age,
Ye meane to make it new againe
  With mighty Rebels rage ;
You shall have much adoe be sure
  Though you thinke nothing so :
You have to long a time sat still
  And suffered truth to growe.

When God and prince is ioynde in one
  For to defende the truth
And you against them stande in fielde,
  Marke then what it ensuth :
The ruine of the contrarie
  Must needes with speede be seene
For troubling still the flocke of Christ
  And such a quiet queene.
What nobles are they that ye have
  With you to take your parts,
They may be noble well by name,
  But farre from noble harts.

Belyke ye would make men in doubt
  That some doe beare the face
To love their prince, and yet at neede
  To turne unto your case.

O hatefull men unto the blouds
  That alwayes bene trewe,
If you have such, then name them out
  From Judas' line, the Jewe.
That they with speede may hang themselves,
  For treason to their Prince,
A doubtfull denne that so blowth out—
  A poysonde nursing stinche.

Such as you be, hir noble grace
  Hath trusted over long,
.For nowe you thinke that in the fielde
  For hir ye are to strong.
It may be so, the nobles mo
  Both fathers and their sonnes
Be puissant men to beare a Crosse
  Out of the noble Nortounes.
You say your faythes is promised
  In this your enterprise,
Eche unto eche, to further forth
  Your meaning good and wise.

What fayth is that what doe you meane?
  When fayth to Prince is broke?
You meane to pull your neckes from tye
  Of gentle princes yoke:

And set yourselves at libertie
  And eke your rowte so rude
So that to royal dignitie
  Eche shall himself intrude
For this ye may right well beleve
  Not woorst in all your ranke
But thinkes himselfe as good as ye,
  And lookes for as much thanke.

You say hir grace is led by such
  As wicked are and evil.
By whom I pray you, are ye led
  I may say, by the Devil.
Whom would ye poynt to leave hir grace?
  If ye might have your choyse
The Pope I thinke, your father chiefe,
  Should have your holy voyse.
And then she should be led indeede,
  As lamb for to be slaine
Wo worth such heades, as so would fee
  Hir grace for all hir paine.

But this I would ye should me tell
  When she came to hir throne,
What was she then of age or wit?
  Give answere every one?

Was not hir age so competent
  And eke hir head so wise
As none that heard, or did hir knowe,
  Could more in hir devise ?
Yea, you yourselves (I dare well say)
  At that same present houre,
Of all the princes farre or neere
  Tooke hir to be the flowre.

And had she not then will and powre
  Hir counsaylers to chuse
To take in whom that she thought good
  And whom she would refuse ?
If ye should paint hir counsaylers
  The case were very straunge.
No marveyle though in deedes ye rove
  When so in wordes ye raunge.
And yet good sirs, this is well knowne
  That nothing hath been ment
And done, in matters of the Church
  But by the Parliament.

Wherein the nobles of the realme
  The Bishop, and the Lorde,
And commons all gave their consent
  And thereto did accorde.

The booke that called is by name
   The booke of common prayer,
Was sent to you by these afore
   Though you would it appaire,
By brutinge forth that perverse men
   Seducers of the Queene,
Hat set it out, O simple men
   What shall I of you deeme ?

Doth not the act that is set out
   Speake to you in this wise ?
Have you not read and seen the same
   And now the same denies ?
Will you that be but private men
   Attempt for to put downe
The thing that was authorised
   By hir that weares the crown ?
What gappe make you to breache of lawe
   If this your fact be good ?
No Parliament, no Prince shall rule,
   But shedding still of blood.

If men may rise against their Prince
   That all things doth by lawe,
Then call for Captain Cobler [1] in
   And wayte upon Jack Strawe.

Ye saye ye feare the noble bloud
　It should be made away
And ye yourselves will do the same
　Of others that you saye,
By force ye say ye will redresse
　The things that are amisse
Where had you that, out of what schoole ?
　Shew me then where it is ;

For in your wordes, there is enclosde
　That will the Queen or no,
You will set up, that she put doune ;
　That so ye meane ye show
If ye be subiects as you say,
　Where learned ye to force ?
But this ye meane (I doe suppose)
　With her to make a Corce.
The mother church you will defende
　What children call ye these,
When trayterously themselves they bende
　Their mother to disease.

But like it is, the mother that
　Ye meane to prop with power,
The spouse of Christ that she is not,
　But antichristes whoore.

For sure I am, the Church of Christ
 Did never knowe this way,
In any place, at any tyme
 Their prince to disobey.
What fathers of the fayth ye bee
 All men may easily judge,
Who is so blinde that cannot see
 How causeless ye doe grudge?

The auncient customes of the Church
 You say you will restore,
The liberties that she hath had
 She shall have as to fore.
You speake but for to make hir smoyle
 Such libertie to have
The prince and realme againe to spoyle
 Of that that once they gave.
The Monke, the Fryer, and eke the Nonne,
 The Armit and the Anker,
You doe intende belyke to place
 In your most holy Ranker.

God send you all as well to speede,
 And make your way as streight,
As such as you had in the dayes
 Of King Henry the eight.

O that he were alive to see
  How you his daughter use,
But he that hath his soule to keepe
  Shall send you shortly newes.
I doe not doubt, fit for your factes
  The ende of Rebels race,
With shamefull deathes to have the ende
  Full fit in such a case.

Good peoples helpe you seem to crave
  To ayde you in your sturre;
Good people will their Princes wrath
  Be fearfull to incurre.
Though you ne recke like bedlem men
  Your life and lande to leese,
Yet shall you finde the contrary,
  And that in all degrees.
If God by you will punishe us,
  Indeede we must obey
And we the better for his stroke,
  Though you be cast away.

For longer than he thinketh good,
  You shall not sure prevaile
And then will he in wrathfull moode
  Strike down both heade and taile.

This is the way to know the foes
  Of God, and eke our Prince,
Which craftily have kept themselves
  And secretly did wince.
Now may the Queene soone finde them out
  Who faythfull be in deede,
And cursed Papistes by this meanes
  Full soone she may out weede,

The hollow harts will now appeare
  And subiects true in harts
Will now like men, both speake and doe
  And lively play their parts.
And to keepe backe that forreyne power
  Should not this lande destroy,
Ye will yourselves it wast, before
  That they shall it annoy.
But how know ye that forreine power
  Would entermeddle heere ?
Be like ye have them wilde thereto
  You love your lande so deere.

And least that they our strength might finde
  When they approch to lande,
You will if you may work the same,
  It weaken to their hande.

The losse of you, if you be slaine
  As fit is for your sinne
Shall leave the fewer in the lande,
  To let the foe come in,
A case it is to fonde to think
  That Straungers should refourme
The thinges amisse within this lande
  And make it to retourne.

What! is it not a monarchie?
  What Prince hath here to doe?
O who so strong that may us greeve,
  If we be true thereto?
A proverb olde, no land there is
  That can this land subdue
If we agree within ourselves,
  And to our land be true.
Was ever lande so governed
  Sith conquest here to fore
As this hath bene in all respeotes
  This IX yeares and more.

What peace, what rest, what quietnesse
  What welth what helth hath reignde
What iustice hath been ministred
  To all that have complainde

Was ever Prince so mercifull
　As this most noble Queene ?
How she hath nursed the Noble bloud
　Is evidently seene.
Whose head from shoulders hath she cut ?
　Though some did it deserve ?
Whom hath she burnt or in iayle
　Caused that they should starve.

If lenity may make men rise
　Or meekenesse gender yre
If cold may cause the coles to burne ?
　Or water kindell fire ?
If adamant may thrust away
　The Iron or the Steele,
Or shining Sun the naked man
　May cause the colde to feele ?
Then may our Queene, Elizabeth,
　Be thought to be the cause
Why these Rebels do go about
　The breaking of hir lawes.

But sure it is, hir humblenesse
　That she hath ever usde,
The captives now most cankerdly
　With treason have abusde.

God save the Queene ye crie alowde
  With weapon stiffe in hande
To trouble hir whose prudent heade
  Hath saved all the lande.
Such glosing wordes, and painted style
  Are fit for foolish heades
Or else for babes, whose infancie
  Doe lyke as leaders leedes.

But now to you the simple sort
  Leave off from taking part
And speede apace unto your home,
  And to your Prince convart.
Afore that God in wrath doe rise
  By Princes furie wrought.
To beate ye downe in fielde by force
  And bring ye all to nought
Doe you suppose, a Princes powre
  Your Captaines may resist,
There is of you can tell ye no
  And if so be they list.

In hir most noble fathers dayes
  When he came with his powre
Have ye forgot when ye were up
  How eche man took his bower

How often in one yeare ye rose
  The Chronicles doth tell,
And yet no boote, ye had no gaine
  Although ye did rebel.
You never hard, nor ever read
  That Rebelles dyd prevayle
And doe you thinke by dente of sworde
  To make your prince to quaile.

Nay make your count, though you do thinke
  That many be as you,
Of popishe mynd, yet shall you finde
  Their hearts to be full true.
And multitudes that doe beleeve
  This love to be full right,
Are ready prest to take hir part
  If you will trye hir might.
But better no : returne in time
  If you hir grace doe loove
And seeke not iustice as your right,
  But doe hir mercie proove.

You cannot poynt, if fielde be fought
  The victorie at wyll,
What gaine shall come unto your part
  When eche doth other kill ?

O simple men why should ye thus
  Despise the quiet state ?
Of this the realme so governed
  As you were in of late !
The realmes about so troubled
  And you in quiet rest,
Who shall the breakers of the same
  Not utterly detest ?

And what if that ye should increase
  (As God forbid the same)
And princes powre with rebels might
  Should runne abrode by fame
Would not the foes that now be still
  Then buskell to come in, ·
When feebled is the land of might
  By broyles that ye begin
Their holinesse and yours is like
  They seeke but for to raine,
And for your making of their way
  You shall of them be slaine,

Therefore take counsell yet in time
  Afore yee go to farre,
Your Queene, your realme, and happie state
  Above all things prefarre.

For make account, ye shall not bring
  The state to you to yeelde,
You shall first fynd the English bloud,
  To lie in many a feelde.
The sonne, the father, ye shall bring
  With dent of sword to stryke
The brother shall the brother meete
  And doe also the lyke.

In princes cause no kith nor kinne
  Affinitie nor blood,
Shall staye the subiect to set out
  To speed both life and good.
With conscience good and fayth full sure,
  Though he be slaine in feelde
Yet shall he as true subiect dye
  And so his soule up yeelde
Whereas if you in fielde be slayne
  Because ye did rebell
By fact, your slaughter hat the waye
  To Devills that are in hell.

Who for because they did arise
  Against the Lord of might,
As you doe now against his powre
  They lost eternall light

D

The fatherlesse that ye shall make
  And widdowes in their wo
Shall pray your fee in torments great
  To be for doing so.
· Yea of your own that you shall leave
  Shall cursse you for your deedes,
When they shall feele the plague to stretch
  To them, for your yll meedes.

Bethink yourselves and take advice
  And speedily repent
Accept the pardon of the Prince
  When it to you is sent.
So may you save your bodies yet
  Your soules and eke your good,
And stay the Devill that hopes by you
  To spill much Christian blood
God save our Queene, and keep in peace
  This Island evermore.
So shall we render unto him
  Eternall thanks therefore.

finis (W. S.)
God save the Queene.

NOTE.—Captain Cobler. Page 15.

[1] A monk of the name of Makarell, assumed the name of Captain Cobler, in the rebellion of the " Pilgrimage of Grace " an important event which has never found an historian, but which is now undertaken by the Author of the Rebellion of 1569—from original documents in the government offices.

LaVergne, TN USA
18 October 2009
161265LV00004B/126/A